The Religion of Man

The Religion of Man

International Edition

Rabindranath Tagore

Foreword by Jon M. Sweeney

Monkfish Book Publishing Company
Rhinebeck, New York

The Religion of Man: International Edition © 2022 by Monkfish Book Publishing Company; Foreword to the Original Monkfish Edition © 2004, 2022 by Philip Novak; Foreword to the New Monkfish Edition © 2022 by Jon M. Sweeney

Paperback ISBN 978-1-948626-55-2
eBook ISBN 978-1-948626-56-9

Library of Congress Cataloging-in-Publication Data

Names: Tagore, Rabindranath, 1861-1941, author. | Sweeney, Jon M., 1967- other.
Title: The religion of man / Rabindranath Tagore ; foreword by Jon M. Sweeney.
Description: International edition. | Rhinebeck, New York : Monkfish Book Publishing Company, [2022] | Includes index.
Identifiers: LCCN 2021045575 (print) | LCCN 2021045576 (ebook) | ISBN 9781948626552 (paperback) | ISBN 9781948626569 (ebook)
Subjects: LCSH: Religion.
Classification: LCC BL50 .T253 2022 (print) | LCC BL50 (ebook) | DDC 200--dc23
LC record available at https://lccn.loc.gov/2021045575
LC ebook record available at https://lccn.loc.gov/2021045576

Book and cover design by Colin Rolfe
Cover photo "Rabindranath Tagore Hindu poet, 1861 - 1941. Photograph, long white beard. Composer of India's national anthem. Nobel Laureate" by Lebrecht Music & Arts / Alarmy Stock Photo

Monkfish Book Publishing Company
22 East Market Street, Suite 304
Rhinebeck, NY 12572
(845) 876-4861
monkfishpublishing.com

Contents

Jon M. Sweeney

Foreword to the New Monkfish Edition

WHEN my interest in Rabindranath Tagore (1861-1941) was fresh a quarter century ago, it seemed that one in four New York City taxi drivers represented the Bangladeshi diaspora. If I figured this out early in a ride, I'd ask my driver, "Do you like Rabindranath Tagore?" The image of their faces lighting up makes me smile still. Tagore is to India and Bangladesh as Shakespeare is to English-dominant countries. Tagore's work is studied by every schoolchild from Gujarat, on the Arabian Sea, to Kolkata, Tagore's birthplace, on the Bay of Bengal. He didn't live to see the separation of Bangladesh from India, in August 1947, but this explains why he's the author of the national anthems of both countries.

He was born in the century of Great Britain's world dominance, and he sometimes supported English rule of his people. He said that they needed education more than revolution. So, for instance, Tagore sometimes criticized the spiritualizing of Gandhi's principle of *satyagraha*, writing: "Passive resistance is a force which is not, in itself, necessarily moral. It can be used against truth as well as for it." The notion that Indians should sacrifice their educations, their families, their very lives for the cause of *satyagraha* was never acceptable to him.

He is still one of the world's best-known poets, and in the East that term "poet" still means something far greater than a writer of verse. His best-known collection, *Gitanjali*, remains in print and is widely read, and sounds at times as if phrases were lifted directly from the King James Bible. "Here is thy footstool," one verse begins. "Thou hast made me endless," begins another. Tagore usually had a hand in translating his work into English. The poems tend to reach only those who are mystically inclined. They speak of God, the soul, and love in ways that other mystical poets such as Kabir and Gibran share. He was also a novelist, playwright, musician, visual artist, philosopher, and author of hundreds of short stories and morality tales. In 1913, Tagore was the first non-European to win the Nobel Prize for Literature.

But most of all, he is remembered for his contributions to religion and politics—the subject of these Hibbert Lectures delivered at Oxford University in 1930.

Familiar with both East and West (he spent years living in Europe and the US), his pedagogy was multilingual, multiethnic, and multicultural. He valued all religious traditions and taught that all people could and should realize the wonders of "the expansion of the human spirit." This shocked protectors of the caste system in which he'd himself been raised a Brahmin.

In *The Religion of Man*, he attempts to overcome barriers between people, and between people of faith, knowing that religion is what often divides us. Much of what he said then seemed to be coming true when he said it, nearly a century ago, and I suspect that he would be shocked to see today how little progress we have made. For instance, he said: "The God of humanity has arrived at the gates of the ruined temple of tribe." Tribes are still thriving, in my experience, and religious people who desire to move beyond them are, from generation to generation, a consistently small percentage of the whole.

Yet, Tagore isn't primarily addressing people involved in organized religion. "Religion" is more broadly conceived by him in ways that make more sense today than I'm sure they made in 1930. Religion is not so much where we go to worship, but what we dream, create, and construct; it is our values and our creativity:

> Each age reveals its personality as dreamer in its great expressions that carry it across surging centuries in the continental plateau of permanent human history. These expressions may not be consciously religious, but.... This consciousness finds it manifestation in science, philosophy and the arts, in social ethics, in all things that carry their ultimate value in themselves. (chapter 3)

Tagore writes as one who has spent a lifetime as an educator, and he urges that we should be increasingly aware of how the natural, human, and divine commingle in the world. The humanity of God and the divinity of human beings are his joint preoccupation. We should develop a sense of wonder that lives beyond childhood and hold within ourselves the kinship and wondrousness of every other human being.

Prophets stand all on an equal plane: Zarathustra, Krishna, Jesus. The ultimate goal of any form of religion should be the life of human beings, and this comes most clearly to us if and when we realize that there is divinity in each one: "It is for us to realize the Person who is in the heart of the All" (chapter 7). This strikes me as deeply Hindu, deeply Jewish, deeply Christian, and so on.

For those who might be tempted to take Tagore's wisdom in the direction of eradicating organized religion in favor of the broader vision of religion alone, take note of how he says, in chapter 13, "Spiritual Freedom," that the greatest cause of misery in our lives is "the obscurity of life's significance." It is the purpose of every religious tradition and religious practitioner to communicate that significance to the world. We need this now and always.

He was a realist and a lover of truth. Embracing the world while standing with both feet firmly planted among his native people earned him the reputation of a prophet. But more importantly, and why I hope you will look past the datedness of the title of this work, Tagore was a profoundly human being. This is a book of hope for a religious future that is at the same time conscious of its cosmic origins and respectful of the needs of people everywhere.

—Jon M. Sweeney
Meister Eckhart's Book of the Heart (coauthor)
Francis of Assisi in His Own Words (translator)
etc.

Philip Novak

Foreword to the Original
Monkfish Edition

"**THE** Real is one; the wise call it by many names." Uttered by an unknown Vedic seer some three thousand years ago, this mighty insight, so ancient and so new, has been the central inspiration for many of India's greatest religious thinkers. When Mother India gave birth to Rabindranath Tagore in 1861, she endowed him, too, with the gift for seeing the One behind and within the many—and much else besides. The scion of a wealthy Calcutta family, Rabindranath showed signs even in childhood of the prodigious literary talent that would characterize his adult life. In his fiftieth year he was awarded the Nobel Prize for Literature—the first Asian ever to have received this honor—and two years later England knighted him. In 1930 Sir Rabindranath delivered the Hibbert Lectures at Oxford which are the substance of this book. His concern is to help us to see what he sees so clearly: that the various religions of humankind are evolving expressions of the one Religion of Humanity, an eternal essence that lies within and beyond humanity's historical religions, drawing the human family steadily forward toward greater and richer realizations of unity, love and freedom.

Sir Rabindranath grew to manhood as Darwin's ideas made their claims upon the world's attention. As the book opens, evolution is much on his mind. Since Darwin there seem to be two kinds of religious thinkers: those who battle evolution as antithetical to God; and those who celebrate evolution as God's most stupendous self-disclosure. If God is too small to encompass evolution, Sir Rabindranath would surely say, it is a failure not of God but of our imagination. His early chapters are lyrical accounts of the cosmic and biological evolutions that shaped the universe prior to human emergence. Out of matter arose life. Yet how is it possible for life to appear out of sheer lifelessness? Can a stream rise higher than its source? Doesn't life's appearance on the evolutionary stage suggest that a deeper Life had been there all the while, awaiting its cue? And in life's immense journey through aeons of time do we not already perceive in its most characteristic impulse—the formation of complex unities—the very mark of love?

And out of life arose mind. Yet how is it possible for mind to arise from sheer mindlessness? Doesn't the appearance of the human mind on the evolutionary stage suggest that a deeper Mind had been there all along, awaiting its cue? For Sir Rabindranath, the emergence of the human mind is the decisive spiritual moment. The material cosmos may be stunning in its immensity but it is marked in its every atom by profound limitation and finitude. Mind introduces a power of which no mere lump of matter can ever dream, a power to imagine and know the boundlessness of God and the freedom of the Infinite. In reaching out for God, human beings overcome themselves. This is the secret of spiritual evolution, and "our soul withers when it has no object of profound interest that demands of it clarity of mind and heroic attention to maintain and nurture it." The task of the poet and the artist is to keep the Infinite before our eyes and to remind us that it ever dwells within our souls.

The "Infinite" sounds remote, cold. Sir Rabindranath surprises us. His "Infinite" is profoundly personal, a unity-in-relationship of all the relationships that constitute the world. The Infinite's freedom is not freedom from relationship but the freedom of relationship, and the royal road to that freedom is the yoga of love. Love anticipates God's freedom because, as every lover knows, when love is truly present it is always 'enough.' Gallingly, Sir Rabindranath defines the Buddha's "nirvana" as the "elimination of all barriers to love." We are related to everyone and everything, if we but knew it. "The consciousness of God transcends the limitations of race and gathers together all human beings within one spiritual circle of union."

The history of human religions on their way to the Religion of Humanity is the record of a groping, uncertain journey, often as terrifying as uplifting. In one of the loveliest passages in the book Sir Rabindranath honors Zarathustra as the first of the great prophets to call human beings away from their long habit of manipulating tribal gods with magic rituals toward the moral self-transformation that is the noblest mode of spiritual life. A glance around our world will suffice to show that this great shift is still very much in progress. We are still calling upon tribal gods in hope of tribal victories. But the Infinite's slow and steady pull gathers us increasingly into the sacred web of relationship where one day each of us will reach out in love toward all others.

"I am a singer," says Sir Rabindranath, "ever attracted by the house of songs." Science gives us facts, but spiritual experience alone engenders the joy that is the surest mark of truth. "All that I feel about religion is from vision and not from knowledge," he says. "I cannot satisfactorily answer any questions about evil, or about what happens after death . . . [All I know is that] my soul has touched the infinite and has become intensely conscious of it through the illumination of joy."

—Philip Novak
Program in Religion and Philosophy
Dept. of Humanities
Dominican University of California
2004

Andrew Robinson

The Religion of Man:
An Introduction

THE *Religion of Man* is the work of a man remarkable by the standard of any age. When Rabindranath Tagore delivered it as a lecture at Oxford in May 1930, at the age of 69, this fact was generally, if not always clearly appreciated, both in India and in the West. Since this is no longer so, nearly half a century after his death, and since his religious ideas spring, by his own admission, entirely from his individual experiences, it may be helpful to the reader to have a brief sketch of his incredibly full life, emphasising those aspects that Tagore himself refers to in his lecture.

'My own ancestors came floating to Calcutta upon the earliest tide of the fluctuating fortune of the East India Company,' he tells us. They were among the first Bengalis to become rich by trade with the British. Dwarkanath Tagore, Rabindranath's grandfather, was one of the richest men in Calcutta, famous for the extravagance of his pleasures, his lack of religious orthodoxy, and his philanthropy. He was among the first Hindus of note to visit Europe, where he entertained royalty and was known as 'Prince' Dwarkanath. He died in London in 1846.

His son Debendranath was sharply different. Until his late teens, he led the self-indulgent life expected of him as the spoilt son of a rich father. It took the lingering death of his grandmother on the banks of the Ganges at Benares, attended by the young man, to alter his whole outlook. He renounced worldliness, and began a search for enlightenment in the literatures of both East and West. A torn page of the Isopanishad, carried to him quite by chance by a passing breeze, determined the future course of his life. In Rabindranath's translation it read:

> Thou must know that whatever moves in this moving world is enveloped by God. And therefore find thy enjoyment in renunciation, never coveting what belongs to others.

Shortly after this, Debendranath revived a religious movement of reformed Hinduism known as the Brahmo Samaj and remained one of its leaders until his death in 1905 at the age of 88. He became known as an austere, saintly figure—the Maharshi, or 'Great Sage'.

Rabindranath, the fourteenth of his children, born in 1861, followed a different path from his grandfather and father from the start. He took after both of them simultaneously. In the words of a poem from *Gitanjali*, the collection that won Tagore the Nobel prize for Literature, 'Deliverance is not for me, and renunciation . . . I feel the embrace of freedom in a thousand bonds of delight.'

His early upbringing contributed; he was confined entirely to school and to the Tagore mansion in North Calcutta, under the control of generally harsh servants and a punishing schedule of lessons. He seldom saw his parents. In the space of seven years he attended four schools with complete lack of academic distinction, hating them all. Both freedom and delight were in short supply and he longed for them.

He read widely at this time, however, stimulated by the diversely talented members of the family, who created an atmosphere of constant artistic and intellectual innovation around him. His first worthwhile poetry appeared in Bengali (like all his poetry), when he was 16, written under a pseudonym, following the example of the eighteenth-century English boy-poet, Thomas Chatterson. By the early 1880s, after a visit to England where he learnt some melodies and seems to have fallen in love but achieved no qualifications, he was established in Bengal as the coming poet. One poem, 'The Awakening of the Waterfall', had been written as the direct result of a vision, 'a sudden spring breeze of religious experience', which Tagore describes vividly.

Political and social issues began to command his attention, too. He launched himself on what would become a lifetime of stern denunciation of the failings of his fellow Bengalis. He also felt an urge to take part in his father's movement and became a secretary of a section of the Brahmo Samaj. This was not a success; Tagore soon realised that his cast of mind could not fit that of a group or institution, whether it be educational, religious or political. His antipathy for such cages of the spirit grew with the passing of time and eventually found expression in his ambivalent feelings towards the school and university he founded, helped by the money he received from his Nobel prize. 'I have my conviction that in religion, and also in the arts, that which is common to a group is not important,' he writes. 'Indeed, very often it is a contagion of mutual imitation.'

From about 1890, at the insistence of Maharshi Debendranath, who feared that his youngest son was out of touch with practical affairs, Rabindanath found himself posted to the family estates in riparian East Bengal as a manager, where he spent much of his time on a houseboat. A fresh phase in his writing began, drawing upon his new awareness of life in rural Bengal away from the hot-house of the Calcutta literati. Some of the short stories he wrote there about the people of the estate are as fine as those of Chekhov and Maupassant, some of his letters to a niece are great works of literature, while his poetry acquired new depth and lyricism.

Around the turn of the century he moved back to West Bengal, to Santiniketan, the beautiful bare stretch of country some hundred miles north-west of Calcutta that the Maharshi had purchased in 1863 as a place of meditation. (The name, given by him, means 'Abode of Peace.') Tagore wanted to found a school there, along the lines of the ancient forest hermitages or *tapovana* who's unhurried purity of purpose had disappeared from modern India. He planned to educate his own children there, away from the Calcutta crammers he had suffered. Despite his lack of finance, and the general skepticism of others, he persevered with the idea. About twenty years later, a university, Visva Bharati, was established too, which attracted pupils from all over India and a number of significant foreign scholars. Its declared aim was characteristic of Tagore:

> to represent India where she has her wealth of mind
> which is for all. Visva Bharati acknowledges India's
> obligation to offer to others the hospitality of her

best culture and India's right to accept from others their best.

A number of well-known Indians have taught and studied there, including the film director Satyajit Ray, who was an art student in the early 1940s, at the time of Tagore's death.

One of the foreigners later founded his own institution in England, the Dartington Trust, inspired by Tagore's example. This was Leonard Elmhirst, the wealthy son of a priest, an agricultural economist whom Tagore met in the USA in 1920. He spent several years around Santiniketan attempting to set up rural development projects, financed by the woman he later married, the American heiress, Dorothy Straight, to whom Tagore dedicated *The Religion of Man*. Elmhirst later became Tagore's travelling companion, and after his death wrote the following description of him:

> I knew him ill and in good health; angry and in the best of spirits and good humour—never was there a more lively and witty or stimulating traveller, and to see a new country with him was a perpetual delight. If you ask me why, I would say that there was no aspect of human existence which did not exercise some fascination for him and around which he did not allow his mind and fertile imagination to play. Where, as a young man, I had been brought up in a world in which the religious and the secular were separate, he insisted that in poetry, music, art and life they were one, that there should be no dividing line.

Precisely such attitudes led Tagore to care deeply about the economic, social, and moral revival of India, but to condemn the political expression of Indian nationalism, first in Bengal in the 1890s onwards, and later under Gandhi. Although he was passionately opposed to the British plan to partition Bengal, which took place in 1905, he was greatly disturbed by the violence that soon followed it. In speeches, essays, short stories, novels and songs in Bengali, he opposed Bengali nationalism, and in 1916 gave the first of many international lecture tours with a similar message in English, to the annoyance of some of his American and Japanese audience. Not long after that he began a series of public and private debates with Gandhi (whom he had dubbed Mahatma—'Great Soul'), about the ethics of non-cooperation. He is no doubt alluding to this when he writes that, 'I know men who preach the cult of simple life by glorifying the spiritual merit of poverty. I refuse to imagine any special value in poverty when it is mere negation.' To Tagore, it was absolutely vital for Indians to maintain a positive approach to the West, despite their mistreatment by the British Raj, and notwithstanding his own courageous stand when news of the Amritsar massacre of April 1919 reached him; he requested the Viceroy to relieve him of his knighthood.

The impact of this gesture was substantial, coming in the wake of his third historic visit to England in 1912-13, the award of the Nobel prize for Literature in 1913, and his tour of Japan and the USA. Between 1920 and 1930, Tagore visited just about every major country in Europe, the USA, the USSR, China and Japan, South-East Asia, and Argentina, often to tumultuous receptions. His motives were a mixture of relent-lessness and curiosity (including a desire to know the western reaction to his unique paintings started when he was 67), a wish to raise money for his school and university, and a growing conviction that he had a role as an ambassador of goodwill between nations, whose physical separation was contracting dramatically as a result of better communications. He had come to believe that 'the vastness of the race problem with which we are faced today will either compel us to train ourselves to moral fitness in the place of merely external efficiency, or the complications arising out of it will fetter all our movement and drag us to our death'.

Trenchantly he describes and diagnoses that 'mentality which is the product of racial isolation' in terms that foreshadow Nazi Germany with chilling clarity, and which still speak forcefully to us today; it is impossible to read him without admiring his prophetic intensity, especially when we are aware of its foundation in first-hand experience. His final address to the world, *Crisis in Civilisation*, delivered just before his eightieth birthday in April 1941, was equally impressive, and also moving; his warnings had gone unheeded, but even as bombs were falling on the cities of Europe that he loved, he did not lose hope in Man.

In *The Religion of Man*, he puts his faith in the right-thinking people he has met around the world in nearly two decades of travelling, a roll-call of eminent artists and thinkers, amongst others, that is a fair testament to the interest he aroused. One of them was Albert Einstein, whom Tagore met in Europe after giving the Hibbert Lectures in England and spending some time in Dartington. In a fascinating conversation, Tagore maintained that the Universe can have no existence that is independent of Man, because the scientific conception of it must be that of the scientific man:

EINSTEIN: Truth, then, or Beauty is not independent of Man?
TAGORE: No.

EINSTEIN: If there were no human beings anymore, the Apollo of Belvedere would no longer be beautiful?

TAGORE: No.

EINSTEIN: I agree to this conception of Beauty, but not with regard to Truth.

TAGORE: Why not? Truth is realised through man.

EINSTEIN: I cannot prove that my conception is right, but that is my religion.

In Tagore's view, Truth is the 'perfect comprehension of the Universal Mind' of Man, a concept that lies at the heart of his religion. He is unshakably convinced of human unity. In one of the beguiling poetic similes in which *The Religion of Man* abounds, he compares the innumerable individuals who compose the history of mankind to the constituent cells of our bodies. From the point of view of a cell, or a human individual, each may appear either separate or connected, but from a wider perspective in time and space they will all appear united. This consciousness of being part of a whole varies greatly from person to person. 'It finds its manifestation' writes Tagore,

> in science, philosophy and the arts, in social ethics,
> in all things that carry their ultimate value in them-
> selves. These are truly spiritual and they should all
> be consciously coordinated in one great religion of
> Man, representing his ceaseless endeavour to reach
> the perfect in great thoughts and deeds and dreams,
> in immortal symbols of art, revealing his aspiration
> for rising in dignity of being.

—**Andrew Robinson**

Rabindranath Tagore

Preface

THE chapters included in this book, which comprises the
Hibbert Lectures delivered in Oxford, at Manchester College,
during the month of May 1930, contain also the gleanings of
my thoughts on the same subject from the harvest of many lectures and addresses delivered in different countries of the world
over a considerable period of my life.

The fact that one theme runs through all only proves to me
that the Religion of Man has been growing within my mind as
a religious experience and not merely as a philosophical subject. In fact, a very large portion of my writings, beginning from
the earlier products of my immature youth down to the present time, carry an almost continuous trace of the history of this
growth. Today I am made conscious of the fact that the works
that I have started and the words that I have uttered are deeply
linked by a unity of inspiration whose proper definition has
often remained unrevealed to me.

In the present volume I offer the evidence of my own personal life brought into a definite focus. To some of my readers this will supply matter of psychological interest; but for others I hope it will carry with it its own ideal value important for such a subject as religion.

My sincere thanks are due to the Hibbert Trustees, and especially to Dr. W. H. Drummond, with whom I have been in constant correspondence, for allowing me to postpone the delivery of these Hibbert Lectures from the year 1928, when I was too ill to proceed to Europe, until the summer of 1930. I have also to thank the Trustees for their very kind permission given to me to present the substance of the lectures in this book in an enlarged form by dividing the whole subject into chapters instead of keeping strictly to the lecture form in which they were delivered in Oxford. May I add that the great kindness of my hostess, Mrs. Drummond, in Oxford will always remain in my memory along with these lectures as intimately associated with them?

In the Appendix I have gathered together from my own writings certain parallel passages which bring the reader to the heart of my main theme. Furthermore, two extracts, which contain historical material of great value, are from the pen of my esteemed colleague and friend, Professor Kshiti Mohan Sen. To him I would express my gratitude for the help he has given me in bringing before me the religious ideas of medieval India which touch the subject of my lectures.

—Rabindranath Tagore
September 1930

The eternal Dream
  is borne on the wings of ageless Light
  that rends the veil of the vague
    and goes across Time
  weaving ceaseless patterns of Being.

The mystery remains dumb,
  the meaning of this pilgrimage,
  the endless adventure of existence
whose rush along the sky
  flames up into innumerable rings of paths,
till at last knowledge gleams out from the dusk
    in the infinity of human spirit,
  and in that dim-lighted dawn
  she speechlessly gazes through the break in the mist
    at the vision of Life and of Love
  emerging from the tumult of profound pain and joy.

Santiniketan,
September 16, 1929
(Composed for the Opening Day Celebrations of the
Indian College, Montpellier, France.)

Chapter I

Man's Universe

LIGHT, as the radiant energy of creation, started the ring-dance of atoms in a diminutive sky, and also the dance of the stars in the vast, lonely theatre of time and space. The planets came out of their bath of fire and basked in the sun for ages. They were the thrones of the gigantic Inert, dumb and desolate, which knew not the meaning of its own blind destiny and majestically frowned upon a future when its monarchy would be menaced.

Then came a time when life was brought into the arena in the tiniest little monocycle of a cell. With its gift of growth and power of adaptation it faced the ponderous enormity of things, and contradicted the unmeaningness of their bulk. It was made conscious not of the volume but of the value of existence, which it ever tried to enhance and maintain in many-branched paths of creation, overcoming the obstructive inertia of Nature by obeying Nature's law.

But the miracle of creation did not stop here in this isolated speck of life launched on a lonely voyage to the Unknown. A multitude of cells were bound together into a larger unit, not through aggregation, but through a marvellous quality of complex inter-relationship maintaining a perfect co-ordination of functions. This is the creative principle of unity, the divine mystery of existence, that baffles all analysis. The larger co-operative units could adequately pay for a greater freedom of self-expression, and they began to form and develop in their bodies new organs of power, new instruments of efficiency. This was the march of evolution ever unfolding the potentialities of life.

But this evolution which continues on the physical plane has its limited range. All exaggeration in that direction becomes a burden that breaks the natural rhythm of life, and those creatures that encouraged their ambitious flesh to grow in dimensions have nearly all perished of their cumbrous absurdity.

Before the chapter ended Man appeared and turned the course of this evolution from an indefinite march of physical aggrandisement to a freedom of a more subtle perfection. This has made possible his progress to become unlimited, and has enabled him to realize the boundless in his power.

The fire is lighted, the hammers are working, and for laborious days and nights amidst dirt and discordance the musical instrument is being made. We may accept this as a detached fact and follow its evolution. But when the music is revealed, we know that the whole thing is a part of the manifestation of music in spite of its contradictory character. The process of evolution, which after ages has reached man, must be realized in its unity with him, though in him it assumes a new value and proceeds to a different path. It is a continuous process that finds its meaning in Man; and we must acknowledge that the evolution which Science talks of is that of Man's universe. The leather binding and title page are parts of the book itself; and this world that we perceive through our senses and mind and life's experience is profoundly one with ourselves.

The divine principle of unity has ever been that of an inner inter-relationship. This is revealed in some of its earliest stages in the evolution of multicellular life on this planet. The most perfect inward expression has been attained by man in his own body. But what is most important of all is the fact that man has also attained its realization in a more subtle body outside his physical system. He misses himself when isolated; he finds his own larger and truer self in his wide human relationship. His multicellular body is born and it dies; his multi-personal humanity is immortal. In this ideal of unity he realizes the eternal in his life and the boundless in his love. The unity becomes not a mere subjective idea, but an energizing truth. Whatever name may be given to it, and whatever form it symbolizes, the consciousness of this unity is spiritual, and our effort to be true to it is our religion. It ever waits to be revealed in our history in a more and more perfect illumination.

We have our eyes, which relate to us the vision of the physical universe. We have also an inner faculty of our own which helps us to find our relationship with the supreme self of man, the universe of personality. This faculty is our luminous imagination, which in its higher stage is special to man. It offers us that vision of wholeness which for the biological necessity of physical survival is superfluous; its purpose is to arouse in us the sense of perfection which is our true sense of immortality. For perfection dwells ideally in Man the Eternal, inspiring love for this ideal in the individual, urging him more and more to realize it.

The development of intelligence and physical power is equally necessary in animals and men for their purposes of living; but what is unique in man is the development of his consciousness which gradually deepens and widens the realization of his immortal being, the perfect, the eternal. It inspires those creations of his that reveal the divinity in him—which is his humanity—in the varied manifestations of truth, goodness and beauty, in the freedom of activity which is not for his use but for his ultimate expression. The individual man must exist for Man the great, and must express him in disinterested works, in science and philosophy, in literature and arts, in service and worship. This is his religion, which is working in the heart of all his religions in various names and forms. He knows and uses this world where it is endless and thus attains greatness, but he realizes his own truth where it is perfect and thus finds his fulfilment.

THE idea of the humanity of our God, or the divinity of Man the Eternal, is the main subject of this book. This thought of God has not grown in my mind through any process of philosophical reasoning. On the contrary, it has followed the current of my temperament from early days until it suddenly flashed into my consciousness with a direct vision. The experience which I have described in one of the chapters which follow convinced me that on the surface of our being we have the ever-changing phases of the individual self, but in the depth there dwells the Eternal Spirit of human unity beyond our direct knowledge. It very often contradicts the trivialities of our daily life, and upsets the arrangements made for securing our personal exclusiveness behind the walls of individual habits and superficial conventions. It inspires in us works that are the expressions of a Universal Spirit; it invokes unexpectedly in the midst of a self-centred life a supreme sacrifice. At its call, we hasten to dedicate our lives to the cause of truth and beauty, to unrewarded service of others, in spite of our lack of faith in the positive reality of the ideal values.

During the discussion of my own religious experience I have expressed my belief that the first stage of my realization was through my feeling of intimacy with Nature—not that Nature which has its channel of information for our mind and physical relationship with our living body, but that which satisfies our personality with manifestations that make our life rich and stimulate our imagination in their harmony of forms, colours, sounds and movements. It is not that world which vanishes into abstract symbols behind its own testimony to Science, but that which lavishly displays its wealth of reality to our personal self having its own perpetual reaction upon our human nature.

I have mentioned in connection with my personal experience some songs which I had often heard from wandering village singers, belonging to a popular sect of Bengal, called Baüls,[1] who have no images, temples, scriptures, or ceremonials, who declare in their songs the divinity of Man, and express for him an intense feeling of love. Coming from men who are unsophisticated, living a simple life in obscurity, it gives us a clue to the inner meaning of all religions. For it suggests that these religions are never about a God of cosmic force, but rather about the God of human personality.

At the same time it must be admitted that even the impersonal aspect of truth dealt with by Science belongs to the human Universe. But men of Science tell us that truth, unlike beauty and goodness, is independent of our consciousness. They explain to us how the belief that truth is independent of the human mind is a mystical belief, natural to man but at the same time inexplicable. But may not the explanation be this, that ideal truth does not depend upon the individual mind of man, but on the universal mind which comprehends the individual? For to say that truth, as we see it, exists apart from humanity is really to contradict Science itself; because Science can only organize into rational concepts those facts which man can know and understand, and logic is a machinery of thinking created by the mechanic man.

The table that I am using with all its varied meanings appears as a table for man through his special organ of senses and his special organ of thoughts. When scientifically analysed the same table offers an enormously different appearance to him from that given by his senses. The evidence of his physical senses and that of his logic and his scientific instruments are both related to his own power of comprehension; both are true and true for him. He makes use of the table with full confidence for his physical purposes, and with equal confidence makes intellectual use of it for his scientific knowledge. But the knowledge is his who is a man. If a particular man as an individual did not exist, the table would exist all the same, but still as a thing that is related to the human mind. The contradiction that there is between the table of our sense perception and the table of our scientific knowledge has its common centre of reconciliation in human personality.

The same thing holds true in the realm of idea. In the scientific idea of the world there is no gap in the universal law of causality. Whatever happens could never have happened otherwise. This is a generalization which has been made possible by a quality of logic which is possessed by the human mind. But this very mind of Man has its immediate consciousness of will within him which *is* aware of its freedom and ever struggles for it. Every day in most of our behaviour we acknowledge its truth; in fact, our conduct finds its best value in its relation to its truth. Thus this has its analogy in our daily behaviour with regard to a table. For whatever may be the conclusion that Science has unquestionably proved about the table, we are amply rewarded when we deal with it as a solid fact and never as a crowd of fluid elements that represent a certain kind of energy. We can also utilize this phenomenon of the measurement. The space represented by a needle when magnified by the microscope may cause us no anxiety as to the number of angels who could be accommodated on its point, or camels which could walk through its eye. In a cinema-picture our vision of time and space can be expanded or condensed merely according to the different technique of the instrument. A seed carries packed in a minute receptacle a future which is enormous in its contents both in time and space. The truth, which is Man, has not emerged out of nothing at a certain point of time, even though seemingly it might have been manifested then. But the manifestation of Man has no end in itself—not even now. Neither did it have its beginning in any particular time we ascribe to it. The truth of Man is in the heart of eternity, the fact of it being evolved through endless ages. If Man's manifestation has round it a background of millions of light-years, still it is his own background. He includes in himself the time, however long, that carries the process of his becoming, and he is related for the very truth of his existence to all things that surround him.

Relationship is the fundamental truth of this world of appearance. Take, for instance, a piece of coal. When we pursue the fact of it to its ultimate composition, substance which seemingly is the most stable element in it vanishes in centres of revolving forces. These are the units, called the elements of carbon, which can further be analysed into a certain number of protons and electrons. Yet these electrical facts are what they are, not in their detachment, but in their inter-relationship, and though possibly some day they themselves may be further analysed, nevertheless the pervasive truth of inter-relation which is manifested in them will remain.

We do not know how these elements, as carbon, compose a piece of coal; all that we can say is that they build up that appearance through a unity of inter-relationship, which unites them not merely in an individual piece of coal, but in a comradeship of creative co-ordination with the entire physical universe.

Creation has been made possible through the continual self-surrender of the unit to the universe. And the spiritual universe of Man is also ever claiming self-renunciation from the individual units. This spiritual process is not so easy as the physical one in the physical world, for the intelligence and will of the units have to be tempered to those of the universal spirit.

It is said in a verse of the Upanishad that this world which is all movement is pervaded by one supreme unity, and therefore true enjoyment can never be had through the satiscaction of greed, but only through the surrender of our individual self to the Universal Self.

There are thinkers who advocate the doctrine of the plurality of worlds, which can only mean that there are worlds that are absolutely unrelated to each other. Even if this were true it could never be proved. For our universe is the sum total of what Man feels, knows, imagines, reasons to be, and of whatever is knowable to him now or in another time. It affects him differently in its different aspects, in its beauty, its inevitable sequence of happenings, its potentiality; and the world proves itself to him only in its varied effects upon his senses, imagination and reasoning mind.

I do not imply that the final nature of the world depends upon the comprehension of the individual person. Its reality is associated with the universal human mind which comprehends all time and all possibilities of realization. And this is why for the accurate knowledge of things we depend upon Science that represents the rational mind of the universal Man, and not upon that of the individual who dwells in a limited range of space and time and the immediate needs of life. And this is why there is such a thing as progress in our civilization; for progress means that there is an ideal perfection which the individual seeks to reach by extending his limits in knowledge, power, love, enjoyment, thus approaching the universal. The most distant star, whose faint message touches the threshold of the most powerful telescopic vision, has its sympathy with the understanding mind of man, and therefore we can never cease to believe that we shall probe further and further into the mystery of their nature. As we know the truth of the stars we know the great comprehensive mind of man.

We must realize not only the reasoning mind, but also the creative imagination, the love and wisdom that belong to the Supreme Person, whose Spirit is over us all, love for whom comprehends love for all creatures and exceeds in depth and strength all other loves, leading to difficult endeavours and martyrdoms that have no other gain than the fulfilment of this love itself.

The *Isha* of our Upanishad, the Super Soul, which permeates all moving things, is the God of this human universe whose mind we share in all our true knowledge, love and service, and whom to reveal in ourselves through renunciation of self is the highest end of life.

[1]See Appendix I.

Chapter II

The Creative Spirit

ONCE, during the improvisation of a story by a young child, I was coaxed to take my part as the hero. The child imagined that I had been shut in a dark room locked from the outside. She asked me, "What will you do for your freedom?" and I answered, "Shout for help". But, however desirable that might be if it succeeded immediately, it would be unfortunate for the story. And thus she in her imagination had to clear the neighbourhood of all kinds of help that my cries might reach. I was compelled to think of some violent means of kicking through this passive resistance; but for the sake of the story the door had to be made of steel. I found a key, but it would not fit, and the child was delighted at the development of the story jumping over obstructions.

Life's story of evolution, the main subject of which is the opening of the doors of the dark dungeon, seems to develop in the same manner. Difficulties were created, and at each offer of an answer the story had to discover further obstacles in order to carry on the adventure. For to come to an absolutely satisfactory conclusion is to come to the end of all things, and in that case the great child would have nothing else to do but to shut her curtain and go to sleep.

The Spirit of Life began her chapter by introducing a simple living cell against the tremendously powerful challenge of the vast Inert. The triumph was thrillingly great which still refuses to yield its secret. She did not stop there, but defiantly courted difficulties, and in the technique of her art exploited an element which still baffles our logic.

This is the harmony of self-adjusting inter-relationship impossible to analyse. She brought close together numerous cell units and, by grouping them into a self-sustaining sphere of cooperation, elaborated a larger unit. It was not a mere agglomeration. The grouping had its caste system in the division of functions and yet an intimate unity of kinship. The creative life summoned a larger army of cells under her command and imparted into them, let us say, a communal spirit that fought with all its might whenever its integrity was menaced.

This was the tree which has its inner harmony and inner movement of life in its beauty, its strength, its sublime dignity of endurance, its pilgrimage to the Unknown through the tiniest gates of reincarnation. It was a sufficiently marvellous achievement to be a fit termination to the creative venture. But the creative genius cannot stop exhausted; more windows have to be opened; and she went out of her accustomed way and brought another factor into her work, that of locomotion. Risks of living were enhanced, offering opportunities to the daring resourcefulness of the Spirit of Life. For she seems to revel in occasions for a fight against the giant Matter, which has rigidly prohibitory immigration laws against all new-corners from Life's shore.

So the fish was furnished with appliances for moving in an element which offered its density for an obstacle. The air offered an even more difficult obstacle in its lightness; but the challenge was accepted, and the bird was gifted with a marvellous pair of wings that negotiated with the subtle laws of the air and found in it a better ally than the reliable soil of the stable earth. The Arctic snow set up its frigid sentinel; the tropical desert uttered in its scorching breath a gigantic "No" against all life's children. But those peremptory prohibitions were defied, and the frontiers, though guarded by a death penalty, were triumphantly crossed.

This process of conquest could be described as progress for the kingdom of life. It journeyed on through one success to another by dealing with the laws of Nature through the help of the invention of new instruments. This field of life's onward march is a field of ruthless competition. Because the material world is the world of quantity, where resources are limited and victory waits for those who have superior facility in their weapons, therefore success in the path of progress for one group most often runs parallel to defeat in another.

It appears that such scramble and fight for opportunities of living among numerous small combatants suggested at last an imperialism of big bulky flesh—a huge system of muscles and bones, thick and heavy coats of armour and enormous tails. The idea of such indecorous massiveness must have seemed natural to life's providence; for the victory in the world of quantity might reasonably appear to depend upon the bigness of dimension. But such gigantic paraphernalia of defence and attack resulted in an utter defeat, the records of which every day are being dug up from the desert sands and ancient mud flats. These represent the fragments that strew the forgotten paths of a great retreat in the battle of existence. For the heavy weight which these creatures carried was mainly composed of bones, hides, shells, teeth and claws that were non-living, and therefore imposed its whole huge pressure upon life that needed freedom and growth for the perfect expression of its own vital nature. The resources for living which the earth offered for her children were recklessly spent by these megalomaniac monsters of an immoderate appetite for the sake of maintaining a cumbersome system of dead burdens that thwarted them in their true progress. Such a losing game has now become obsolete. To the few stragglers of that party, like the rhinoceros or the hippopotamus, has been allotted a very small space on this earth, absurdly inadequate to their formidable strength and magnitude of proportions, making them look forlornly pathetic in the sublimity of their incongruousness. These and their extinct forerunners have been the biggest failures in life's experiments. And then, on some obscure dusk of dawn, the experiment entered upon a completely new phase of a disarmament proposal, when little Man made his appearance in the arena, bringing with him expectations and suggestions that are unfathomably great.

We must know that the evolution process of the world has made its progress towards the revelation of its *truth*—that is to say some inner value which is not in the extension in space and duration in time. When life came out it did not bring with it any new materials into existence. Its elements are the same which are the materials for the rocks and minerals. Only it evolved a value in them which cannot be measured and analysed. The same thing is true with regard to mind and the consciousness of self; they are revelations of a great meaning, the self-expression of a truth. In man this truth has made its positive appearance, and is struggling to make its manifestation more and more clear.

That which is eternal is realizing itself in history through the obstructions of limits.

The physiological process in the progress of Life's evolution seems to have reached its finality in man. We cannot think of any noticeable addition or modification in our vital instruments which we are likely to allow to persist. If any individual is born, by chance, with an extra pair of eyes or ears, or some unexpected limbs like stowaways without passports, we are sure to do our best to eliminate them from our bodily organization. Any new chance of a too obviously physical variation is certain to meet with a determined disapproval from man, the most powerful veto being expected from his aesthetic nature, which peremptorily refuses to calculate advantage when its majesty is offended by any sudden licence of form. We all know that the back of our body has a wide surface practically unguarded. From the strategic point of view this oversight is unfortunate, causing us annoyances and indignities, if nothing worse, through unwelcome intrusions. And this could reasonably justify in our minds regret for retrenchment in the matter of an original tail, whose memorial we are still made to carry in secret. But the least attempt at the rectification of the policy of economy in this direction is indignantly resented. I strongly believe that the idea of ghosts had its best chance with our timid imagination in our sensitive back—a field of dark ignorance; and yet it is too late for me to hint that one of our eyes could profitably have been spared for our burden-carrier back, so unjustly neglected and haunted by undefined fears.

Thus, while all innovation is stubbornly opposed, there is every sign of a comparative carelessness about the physiological efficiency of the human body. Some of our organs are losing their original vigour. The civilized life, within walled enclosures, has naturally caused in man a weakening of his power of sight and hearing along with subtle sense of the distant. Because of our habit of taking cooked food we give less employment to our teeth and a great deal more to the dentist. Spoilt and pampered by clothes, our skin shows lethargy in its function of adjustment to the atmospheric temperature and in its power of quick recovery from hurts.

The adventurous Life appears to have paused at a crossing in her road before Man came. It seems as if she became aware of wastefulness in carrying on her experiments and adding to her inventions purely on the physical plane. It was proved in Life's case that four is not always twice as much as two. In living things it is necessary to keep to the limit of the perfect unit within which the inter-relationship must not be inordinately strained. The ambition that seeks power in the augmentation of dimension is doomed; for that perfection which is in the inner quality of harmony becomes choked when quantity overwhelms it in a fury of extravagance. The combination of an exaggerated nose and arm that an elephant carries hanging down its front has its advantage. This may induce us to imagine that it would double the advantage for the animal if its tail also could grow into an additional trunk. But the progress which greedily allows Life's field to be crowded with an excessive production of instruments becomes a progress towards death. For Life has its own natural rhythm which a multiplication table has not; and proud progress that rides roughshod over Life's cadence kills it at the end with encumbrances that are unrhythmic. As I have already mentioned, such disasters did happen in the history of evolution.

The moral of that tragic chapter is that if the tail does not have the decency to know where to stop, the drag of this dependency becomes fatal to the body's empire.

Moreover, evolutionary progress on the physical plane inevitably tends to train up its subjects into specialists. The camel is a specialist of the desert and is awkward in the swamp. The hippopotamus which specializes in the mudlands of the Nile is helpless in the neighbouring desert. Such one-sided emphasis breeds professionalism in Life's domain, confining special efficiencies in narrow compartments. The expert training in the aerial sphere is left to the bird; that in the marine is particularly monopolized by the fish. The ostrich is an expert in its own region and would look utterly foolish in an eagle's neighbourhood. They have to remain permanently content with advantages that desperately cling to their limits. Such mutilation of the complete ideal of life for the sake of some exclusive privilege of power is inevitable; for that form of progress deals with materials that are physical and therefore necessarily limited.

To rescue her own career from such a multiplying burden of the dead and such constriction of specialization seems to have been the object of the Spirit of Life at one particular stage. For it does not take long to find out that an indefinite pursuit of quantity creates for Life, which is essentially qualitative, complexities that lead to a vicious circle. These primeval animals that produced an enormous volume of flesh had to build a gigantic system of bones to carry the burden. This required in its turn a long and substantial array of tails to give it balance. Thus their bodies, being compelled to occupy a vast area, exposed a very large surface which had to be protected by a strong, heavy and capacious armour. A progress which represented a congress of dead materials required a parallel organization of teeth and claws, or horns and hooves, which also were dead.

In its own manner one mechanical burden links itself to other burdens of machines, and Life grows to be a carrier of the dead, a mere platform for machinery, until it is crushed to death by its interminable paradoxes. We are told that the greater part of a tree is dead matter; the big stem, except for a thin covering, is lifeless. The tree uses it as a prop in its ambition for a high position and the lifeless timber is the slave that carries on its back the magnitude of the tree. But such a dependence upon a dead dependant has been achieved by the tree at the cost of its real freedom. It had to seek the stable alliance of the earth for the sharing of its burden, which it did by the help of secret underground entanglements making itself permanently stationary.

But the form of life that seeks the great privilege of movement must minimize its load of the dead and must realize that life's progress should be a perfect progress of the inner life itself and not of materials and machinery; the non-living must not continue outgrowing the living, the armour deadening the skin, the armament laming the arms.

At last, when the Spirit of Life found her form in Man, the effort she had begun completed its cycle, and the truth of her mission glimmered into suggestions which dimly pointed to some direction of meaning across her own frontier. Before the end of this cycle was reached, all the suggestions had been external. They were concerned with technique, with life's apparatus, with the efficiency of the organs. This might have exaggerated itself into an endless boredom of physical progress. It can be conceded that the eyes of the bee possessing numerous facets may have some uncommon advantage which we cannot even imagine, or the glow-worm that carries an arrangement for producing light in its person may baffle our capacity and comprehension. Very likely there are creatures having certain organs that give them sensibilities which we cannot have the power to guess.

All such enhanced sensory powers merely add to the mileage in life's journey on the same road lengthening an indefinite distance. They never take us over the border of physical existence.

The same thing may be said not only about life's efficiency, but also life's ornaments. The colouring and decorative patterns on the bodies of some of the deep sea creatures make us silent with amazement. The butterfly's wings, the beetle's back, the peacock's plumes, the shells of the crustaceans, the exuberant outbreak of decoration in plant life, have reached a standard of perfection that seems to be final. And yet if it continues in the same physical direction, then, however much variety of surprising excellence it may produce, it leaves out some great element of unuttered meaning. These ornaments are like ornaments lavished upon a captive girl, luxuriously complete within a narrow limit, speaking of a homesickness for a faraway horizon of emancipation, for an inner depth that is beyond the ken of the senses. The freedom in the physical realm is like the circumscribed freedom in a cage. It produces a proficiency which is mechanical and a beauty which is of the surface. To whatever degree of improvement bodily strength and skill may be developed they keep life tied to a persistence of habit. It is closed, like a mould, useful though it may be for the sake of safety and precisely standardized productions. For centuries the bee repeats its hive, the weaver-bird its nest, the spider its web; and instincts strongly attach themselves to some invariable tendencies of muscles and nerves never being allowed the privilege of making blunders. The physical functions, in order to be strictly reliable, behave like some model schoolboy, obedient, regular, properly repeating lessons by rote, without mischief or mistake in his conduct, but also without spirit and initiative. It is the flawless perfection of rigid limits, a cousin—possibly a distant cousin—of the inanimate.

Instead of allowing a full paradise of perfection to continue its tame and timid rule of faultless regularity the Spirit of Life boldly declared for a further freedom and decided to eat of the fruit of the Tree of Knowledge. This time her struggle was not against the Inert, but against the limitation of her own over-burdened agents. She fought against the tutelage of her prudent old prime minister, the faithful instinct. She adopted a novel method of experiment, promulgated new laws, and tried her hand at moulding Man through a history which was immensely different from that which went before. She took a bold step in throwing open her gates to a dangerously explosive factor which she had cautiously introduced into her council—the element of Mind. I should not say that it was ever absent, but only that at a certain stage some curtain was removed and its play was made evident, even like the dark heat which in its glowing intensity reveals itself in a contradiction of radiancy.

Essentially qualitative, like life itself, the Mind does not occupy space. For that very reason it has no bounds in its mastery of space. Also, like Life, Mind has its meaning in freedom, which it missed in its earliest dealings with Life's children. In the animal, though the mind is allowed to come out of the immediate limits of livelihood, its range is restricted, like the freedom of a child that might run out of its room but not out of the house; or, rather, like the foreign ships to which only a certain port was opened in Japan in the beginning of her contact with the

West in fear of the danger that might befall if the strangers had their uncontrolled opportunity of communication. Mind also is a foreign element for Life; its laws are different, its weapons powerful, its moods and manners most alien.

Like Eve of the Semitic mythology, the Spirit of Life risked the happiness of her placid seclusion to win her freedom. She listened to the whisper of a tempter who promised her the right to a new region of mystery, and was urged into a permanent alliance with the stranger. Up to this point the interest of life was the sole interest in her own kingdom, but another most powerfully parallel interest was created with the advent of this adventurer Mind from an unknown shore. Their interests clash, and complications of a serious nature arise. I have already referred to some vital organs of Man that are suffering from neglect. The only reason has been the diversion created by the Mind interrupting the sole attention which Life's functions claimed in the halcyon days of her undisputed monarchy. It is no secret that Mind has the habit of asserting its own will for its expression against life's will to live and enforcing sacrifices from her. When lately some adventurers accepted the dangerous enterprise to climb Mount Everest, it was solely through the instigation of the arch-rebel Mind. In this case Mind denied its treaty of co-operation with its partner and ignored Life's claim to help in her living. The immemorial privileges of the ancient sovereignty of Life are too often flouted by the irreverent Mind; in fact, all through the course of this alliance there are constant cases of interference with each other's functions, often with unpleasant and even fatal results. But in spite of this, or very often because of this antagonism, the new current of Man's evolution is bringing a wealth to his harbour infinitely beyond the dream of the creatures of monstrous flesh.

The manner in which Man appeared in Life's kingdom was in itself a protest and a challenge, the challenge of Jack to the giant. He carried in his body the declaration of mistrust against the crowding of burdensome implements of physical progress. His Mind spoke to the naked man, "Fear not"; and he stood alone facing the menace of a heavy brigade of formidable muscles. His own puny muscles cried out in despair, and he had to invent for himself in a novel manner and in a new spirit of evolution. This at once gave him his promotion from the passive destiny of the animal to the aristocracy of Man. He began to create his further body, his outer organs—the workers which served him and yet did not directly claim a share of his life. Some of the earliest in his list were bows and arrows. Had this change been undertaken by the physical process of evolution, modifying his arms in a slow and gradual manner, it might have resulted in burdensome and ungainly apparatus. Possibly, however, I am unfair, and the dexterity and grace which Life's technical instinct possesses might have changed his arm into a shooting medium in a perfect manner and with a beautiful form. In that case our lyrical literature to-day would have sung in praise of its fascination, not only for a consummate skill in hunting victims, but also for a similar mischief in a metaphorical sense. But even in the service of lyrics it would show some limitation. For instance, the arms that would specialize in shooting would be awkward in wielding a pen or stringing a lute. But the great advantage in the latest method of human evolution lies in the fact that Man's additional new limbs, like bows and arrows, have become detached. They never tie his arms to any exclusive advantage of efficiency.

The elephant's trunk, the tiger's paws, the claws of the mole, have combined their best expressions in the human arms, which are much weaker in their original capacity than those limbs I have mentioned. It would have been a hugely cumbersome practical joke if the combination of animal limbs had had a simultaneous location in the human organism through some overzeal in biological inventiveness.

The first great economy resulting from the new programme was the relief of the physical burden, which means the maximum efficiency with the minimum pressure of taxation upon the vital resources of the body. Another mission of benefit was this, that it absolved the Spirit of Life in Man's case from the necessity of specialization for the sake of limited success. This has encouraged Man to dream of the possibility of combining in his single person the fish, the bird and the fleet-footed animal that walks on land. Man desired in his completeness to be the one great representative of multiform life, not through wearisome subjection to the haphazard gropings of natural selection, but by the purposeful selection of opportunities with the help of his reasoning mind. It enables the schoolboy who is given a penknife on his birthday to have the advantage over the tiger in the fact that it does not take him a million years to obtain its possession, nor another million years for its removal, when the instrument proves unnecessary or dangerous. The human mind has compressed ages into a few years for the acquisition of steel-made claws. The only cause of anxiety is that the instrument and the temperament which uses it may not keep pace in perfect harmony. In the tiger, the claws and the temperament which only a tiger should possess have had a synchronous development, and in no single tiger is any maladjustment possible between its nails and its tigerliness. But the human boy who grows a claw in the form of a penknife may not at the same time develop the proper temperament necessary for its use which only a man ought to have. The new organs that today are being added as a supplement to Man's original vital stock are too quick and too numerous for his inner nature to develop its own simultaneous concordance with them, and thus we see everywhere innumerable schoolboys in human society playing pranks with their own and other people's lives and welfare by means of newly acquired penknives which have not had time to become humanized.

One thing, I am sure, must have been noticed—that the original plot of the drama is changed, and the mother Spirit of Life has retired into the background, giving full prominence, in the third act, to the Spirit of Man—though the dowager queen, from her inner apartment, still renders necessary help. It is the consciousness in Man of his own creative personality which has ushered in this new regime in Life's kingdom. And from now onwards Man's attempts are directed fully to capture the government and make his own Code of Legislation prevail without a break. We have seen in India those who are called mystics, impatient of the continued regency of Mother Nature in their own body, winning for their will by a concentration of inner forces the vital regions with which our masterful minds have no direct path of communication.

But the most important fact that has come into prominence along with the change of direction in our evolution, is the possession of a Spirit which has its enormous capital with a surplus far in excess of the requirements of the biological animal in Man. Some overflowing influence led us over the strict boundaries of living, and offered to us an open space where Man's thoughts and dreams could have their holidays. Holidays are for gods who have their joy in creation. In Life's primitive paradise, where the mission was merely to live, any luck which came to the creatures entered in from outside by the donations of chance; they lived on perpetual charity, by turns petted and kicked on the back by physical Providence. Beggars never can have harmony among themselves; they are envious of one another, mutually suspicious, like dogs living upon their master's favour, showing their teeth, growling, barking, trying to tear one another. This is what Science describes as the struggle for existence. This beggars' paradise lacked peace; I am sure the suitors for special favour from fate lived in constant preparedness, inventing and multiplying armaments.

But above the din of the clamour and scramble rises the voice of the Angel of Surplus, of leisure, of detachment from the compelling claim of physical need, saying to men, "Rejoice". From his original serfdom as a creature Man takes his right seat as a creator. Whereas, before, his incessant appeal has been to get, now at last the call comes to him to give. His God, whose help he was in the habit of asking, now stands Himself at his door and asks for his offerings. As an animal, he is still dependent upon Nature; as a Man, he is a sovereign who builds his world and rules it.

And there, at this point, comes his religion, whereby he realizes himself in the perspective of the infinite. There is a remarkable verse in the Atharva Veda which says: "Righteousness, truth, great endeavours, empire, religion, enterprise, heroism and prosperity, the past and the future, dwell in the surpassing strength of the surplus."

What is purely physical has its limits like the shell of an egg; the liberation is there in the atmosphere of the infinite, which is indefinable, invisible. Religion can have no meaning in the enclosure of mere physical or material interest; it is in the surplus we carry around our personality—the surplus which is like the atmosphere of the earth, bringing to her a constant circulation of light and life and delightfulness.

I have said in a poem of mine that when the child is detached from its mother's womb it finds its mother in a real relationship whose truth is in freedom. Man in his detachment has realized himself in a wider and deeper relationship with the universe. In his moral life he has the sense of his obligation and his freedom at the same time, and this is goodness. In his spiritual life his sense of the union and the will which is free has its culmination in love. The freedom of opportunity he wins for himself in Nature's region by uniting his power with Nature's forces. The freedom of social relationship he attains through owning responsibility to his community, thus gaining its collective power for his own welfare. In the freedom of consciousness he realizes the sense of his unity with his larger being, finding fulfilment in the dedicated life of an ever-progressive truth and ever-active love.

The first detachment achieved by Man is physical. It represents his freedom from the necessity of developing the power of his senses and limbs in the limited area of his own physiology, having for itself an unbounded background with an immense result in consequence. Nature's original intention was that Man should have the allowance of his sight-power ample enough for his surroundings and a little over. But to have to develop an astronomical telescope on our skull would cause a worse crisis of bankruptcy than it did to the Mammoth whose densely foolish body indulged in an extravagance of tusks. A snail carries its house on its back and therefore the material, the shape and the weight have to be strictly limited to the capacity of the body. But fortunately Man's house need not grow on the foundation of his bones and occupy his flesh. Owing to this detachment, his ambition knows no check to its daring in the dimension and strength of his dwellings. Since his shelter does not depend upon his body, it survives him. This fact greatly affects the man who builds a house, generating in his mind a sense of the eternal in his creative work. And this background of the boundless surplus of time encourages architecture, which seeks a universal value overcoming the miserliness of the present need.

I have already mentioned a stage which Life reached when the units of single cells formed themselves into larger units, each consisting of a multitude. It was not merely an aggregation, but had a mysterious unity of inter-relationship, complex in character, with differences within of forms and function. We can never know concretely what this relation means. There are gaps between the units, but they do not stop the binding force that permeates the whole. There is a future for the whole which is in its growth, but in order to bring this about each unit works and dies to make room for the next worker. While the unit has the right to claim the glory of the whole, yet individually it cannot share the entire wealth that occupies a history yet to be completed.

Of all creatures Man has reached that multi-cellular character in a perfect manner, not only in his body but in his personality. For centuries his evolution has been the evolution of a consciousness that tries to be liberated from the bounds of individual separateness and to comprehend in its relationship a wholeness which may be named Man. This relationship, which has been dimly instinctive, is ever struggling to be fully aware of itself. Physical evolution sought for efficiency in a perfect communication with the physical world; the evolution of Man's consciousness sought for truth in a perfect harmony with the world of personality.

There are those who will say that the idea of humanity is an abstraction, subjective in character. It must be confessed that the concrete objectiveness of this living truth cannot be proved to its own units. They can never see its entireness from outside; for they are one with it. The individual cells of our body have their separate lives; but they never have the opportunity of observing the body as a whole with its past, present and future. If these cells have the power of reasoning (which they may have for aught we know) they have the right to argue that the idea of the body has no objective foundation in fact, and though there is a mysterious sense of attraction and mutual influence running through them, these are nothing positively real; the sole reality which is provable is in the isolation of these cells made by gaps that can never be crossed or bridged.

We know something about a system of explosive atoms whirling separately in a space which is immense compared to their own dimension. Yet we do not know why they should appear to us a solid piece of radiant mineral And if there is an onlooker who at one glance can have the view of the immense time and space occupied by innumerable human individuals engaged in evolving a common history, the positive truth of their solidarity will be concretely evident to him and not the negative fact of their separateness.

The reality of a piece of iron is not provable if we take the evidence of the atom; the only proof is that I see it as a bit of iron, and that it has certain reactions upon my consciousness. Any being from, say, Orion, who has the sight to see the atoms and not the iron, has the right to say that we human beings suffer from an age-long epidemic of hallucination. We need not quarrel with him but go on using the iron as it appears to us. Seers there have been who have said "*Vedabametam*", "I see", and lived a life according to that vision. And though our own sight may be blind we have ever bowed our head to them in reverence.

However, whatever name our logic may give to the truth of human unity, the fact can never be ignored that we have our greatest delight when we realize ourselves in others, and this is the definition of love. This love gives us the testimony of the great whole, which is the complete and final truth of man. It offers us the immense field where we can have our release from the sole monarchy of hunger, of the growling voice, snarling teeth and tearing claws, from the dominance of the limited material means, the source of cruel envy and ignoble deception, where the largest wealth of the human soul has been produced through sympathy and co-operation; through disinterested pursuit of knowledge that recognizes no limit and is unafraid of all time-honoured *tabus*; through a strenuous cultivation of intelligence for service that knows no distinction of colour and clime. The Spirit of Love, dwelling in the boundless realm of the surplus, emancipates our consciousness from the illusory bond of the separateness of self; it is ever trying to spread its illumination in the human world. This is the spirit of civilization, which in all its best endeavour invokes our supreme Being for the only bond of unity that leads us to truth, namely, that of righteousness:

Ya eko varno bahudha saktiyogat
varnan anekan nihitartho dadhati
vichaitti chante viavamadau sa devah
sa no budhya subhaya samyunaktu.

"He who is one, above all colours, and who with his manifold power supplies the inherent needs of men of all colours, who is in the beginning and in the end of the world, is divine, and may he unite us in a relationship of good will."

Chapter III

The Surplus in Man

THERE are certain verses from the Atharva Veda in which the poet discusses his idea of Man, indicating some transcendental meaning that can be translated as follows:

> "Who was it that imparted form to man, gave him majesty, movement, manifestation and character, inspired him with wisdom, music and dancing? When his body was raised upwards he found also the oblique sides and all other directions in him—he who is the Person, the citadel of the infinite being."

Tasmad vai vidvan purushamidan brahmeti manyate.

> "And therefore the wise man knoweth this person as Brahma."

Sanatanam enam ahur utadya syat punarnavah.

"Ancient they call him, and yet he is renewed even now to-day."

In the very beginning of his career Man asserted in his bodily structure his first proclamation of freedom against the established rule of Nature. At a certain bend in the path of evolution he refused to remain a four-footed creature, and the position which he made his body to assume carried with it a permanent gesture of insubordination. For there could be no question that it was Nature's own plan to provide all land-walking mammals with two pairs of legs, evenly distributed along their lengthy trunk heavily weighted with a head at the end. This was the amicable compromise made with the earth when threatened by its conservative downward force, which extorts taxes for all movements. The fact that man gave up such an obviously sensible arrangement proves his inborn mania for repeated reforms of constitution, for pelting amendments at every resolution proposed by Providence.

If we found a four-legged table stalking about upright upon two of its stumps, the remaining two foolishly dangling by its sides, we should be afraid that it was either a nightmare or some supernormal caprice of that piece of furniture, indulging in a practical joke upon the carpenter's idea of fitness. The like absurd behaviour of Man's anatomy encourages us to guess that he was born under the influence of some comet of contradiction, that forces its eccentric path against orbits regulated by Nature. And it is significant that Man should persist in his foolhardiness, in spite of the penalty he pays for opposing the orthodox rule of animal locomotion. He reduces by half the help of an easy balance of his muscles. He is ready to pass his infancy tottering through perilous experiments in making progress upon insufficient support, and followed all through his life by liability to sudden downfalls resulting in tragic or ludicrous consequences from which law-abiding quadrupeds are free. This was his great venture, the relinquishment of a secure position of his limbs, which he could comfortably have retained in return for humbly salaaming the all-powerful dust at every step.

This capacity to stand erect has given our body its freedom of posture, making it easy for us to turn on all sides and realize ourselves at the centre of things. Physically, it symbolizes the fact that while animals have for their progress the prolongation of a narrow line Man has the enlargement of a circle. As a centre he finds his meaning in a wide perspective, and realizes himself in the magnitude of his circumference.

As one freedom leads to another, Man's eyesight also found a wider scope. I do not mean any enhancement of its physical power, which in many predatory animals has a better power of adjustment to light. But from the higher vantage of our physical watch-tower we have gained our *view*, which is not merely information about the location of things but their interrelation and their unity.

But the best means of the expression of his physical freedom gained by Man in his vertical position is through the emancipation of his hands. In our bodily organization these have attained the highest dignity for their skill, their grace, their useful activities, as well as for those that are above all uses. They are the most detached of all our limbs. Once they had their menial vocation as our carriers, but raised from their position as *shudras*, they at once attained responsible status as our helpers. When instead of keeping them underneath us we offered them their place at our side, they revealed capacities that helped us to cross the boundaries of animal nature.

This freedom of view and freedom of action have been accompanied by an analogous mental freedom in Man through his imagination, which is the most distinctly human of all our faculties. It is there to help a creature who has been left unfinished by his designer, undraped, undecorated, unarmoured and without weapons, and, what is worse, ridden by a Mind whose energies for the most part are not tamed and tempered into some difficult ideal of completeness upon a background which is bare. Like all artists he has the freedom to make mistakes, to launch into desperate adventures contradicting and torturing his psychology or physiological normality. This freedom is a divine gift lent to the mortals who are untutored and undisciplined; and therefore the path of their creative progress is strewn with debris of devastation, and stages of their perfection haunted by apparitions of startling deformities. But, all the same, the very training of creation ever makes clear an aim which cannot be in any isolated freak of an individual mind or in that which is only limited to the strictly necessary.

Just as our eyesight enables us to include the individual fact of ourselves in the surrounding view, our imagination makes us intensely conscious of a life we must live which transcends the individual life and contradicts the biological meaning of the instinct of self-preservation. It works at the surplus, and extending beyond the reservation plots of our daily life, builds there the guest chambers of priceless value to offer hospitality to the world-spirit of Man. We have such an honoured right to be the host when our spirit is a free spirit not chained to the animal self. For free spirit is godly and alone can claim kinship with God.

Every true freedom that we may attain in any direction broadens our path of self-realization, which is in superseding the self. The unimaginative repetition of life within a safe restriction imposed by Nature may be good for the animal, but never for Man, who has the responsibility to outlive his life in order to live in truth.

And freedom in its process of creation gives rise to perpetual suggestions of something further than its obvious purpose. For freedom is for expressing the infinite; it imposes limits in its works, not to keep them in permanence but to break them over and over again, and to reveal the endless in unending surprises. This implies a history of constant regeneration, a series of fresh beginnings and continual challenges to the old in order to reach a more and more perfect harmony with some fundamental ideal of truth.

Our civilization, in the constant struggle for a great Further, runs through abrupt chapters of spasmodic divergences. It nearly always begins its new ventures with a cataclysm; for its changes are not mere seasonal changes of ideas gliding through varied periods of flowers and fruit. They are surprises lying in ambuscade provoking revolutionary adjustments. They are changes in the dynasty of living ideals—the ideals that are active in consolidating their dominion with strongholds of physical and mental habits, of symbols, ceremonials and adornments. But however violent may be the revolutions happening in whatever time or country, they never completely detach themselves from a common centre. They find their places in a history which is one.

The civilizations evolved in India or China, Persia or Judaea, Greece or Rome, are like several mountain peaks having different altitude, temperature, flora and fauna, and yet belonging to the same chain of hills. There are no absolute barriers of communication between them; their foundation is the same and they affect the meteorology of an atmosphere which is common to us all. This is at the root of the meaning of the great teacher who said he would not seek his own salvation if all men were not saved; for we all belong to a divine unity, from which our great-souled men have their direct inspiration; they feel it immediately in their own personality, and they proclaim in their life, "I am one with the Supreme, with the Deathless, with the Perfect".

Man, in his mission to create himself, tries to develop in his mind an image of his truth according to an idea which he believes to be universal, and is sure that any expression given to it will persist through all time. This is a mentality absolutely superfluous for biological existence. It represents his struggle for a life which is not limited to his body. For our physical life has its thread of unity in the memory of the past, whereas this ideal life dwells in the prospective memory of the future. In the records of past civilizations, unearthed from the closed records of dust, we find pathetic efforts to make their memories uninterrupted through the ages, like the effort of a child who sets adrift on a paper boat his dream of reaching the distant unknown. But why is this desire? Only because we feel instinctively that in our ideal life we must touch all men and all times through the manifestation of a truth which is eternal and universal. And in order to give expression to it materials are gathered that are excellent and a manner of execution that has a permanent value. For we mortals must offer homage to the Man of the everlasting life. In order to do so, we are expected to pay a great deal more than we need for mere living, and in the attempt we often exhaust our very means of livelihood, and even life itself.

The ideal picture which a savage imagines of himself requires glaring paints and gorgeous fineries, a rowdiness in ornaments and even grotesque deformities of over-wrought extravagance.

He tries to sublimate his individual self into a manifestation which he believes to have the majesty of the ideal Man. He is not satisfied with what he is in his natural limitations; he irresistibly feels something beyond the evident fact of himself which only could give him worth. It is the principle of power, which, according to his present mental stage, is the meaning of the universal reality whereto he belongs, and it is his pious duty to give expression to it even at the cost of his happiness. In fact, through it he becomes one with his God, for him his God is nothing greater than power. The savage takes immense trouble, and often suffers tortures, in order to offer in himself a representation of power in conspicuous colours and distorted shapes, in acts of relentless cruelty and intemperate bravado of self-indulgence. Such an appearance of rude grandiosity evokes a loyal reverence in the members of his community and a fear which gives them an aesthetic satisfaction because it illumi-nates for them the picture of a character which, as far as they know, belongs to ideal humanity. They wish to see in him not an individual, but the Man in whom they all are represented. Therefore, in spite of their sufferings, they enjoy being over-whelmed by his exaggerations and dominated by a will fearfully evident owing to its magnificent caprice in inflicting injuries. They symbolize their idea of unlimited wilfulness in their gods by ascribing to them physical and moral enormities in their ana-tomical idiosyncrasy and virulent vindictiveness crying for the blood of victims, in personal preferences indiscriminate in the choice of recipients and methods of rewards and punishments. In fact, these gods could never be blamed for the least wavering in their conduct owing to any scrupulousness accompanied by the emotion of pity so often derided as sentimentalism by virile intellects of the present day.

However crude all this may be, it proves that Man has a feeling that he is truly represented in something which exceeds himself. He is aware that he is not imperfect, but incomplete. He knows that in himself some meaning has yet to be realized. We do not feel the wonder of it, because it seems so natural to us that barbarism in Man is not absolute, that its limits are like the limits of the horizon. The call is deep in his mind—the call of his own inner truth, which is beyond his direct knowledge and analytical logic. And individuals are born who have no doubt of the truth of this transcendental Man. As our consciousness more and more comprehends it, new valuations are developed in us, new depths and delicacies of delight, a sober dignity of expression through elimination of tawdriness, of frenzied emotions, of all violence in shape, colour, words, or behaviour, of the dark mentality of Ku-Klux-Klanism.

Each age reveals its personality as dreamer in its great expressions that carry it across surging centuries to the continental plateau of permanent human history. These expressions may not be consciously religious, but indirectly they belong to Man's religion. For they are the outcome of the consciousness of the greater Man in the individual men of the race. This consciousness finds its manifestation in science, philosophy and the arts, in social ethics, in all things that carry their ultimate value in themselves. These are truly spiritual and they should all be consciously co-ordinated in one great religion of Man, representing his ceaseless endeavour to reach the perfect in great thoughts and deeds and dreams, in immortal symbols of art, revealing his aspiration for rising in dignity of being.

I had the occasion to visit the ruins of ancient Rome, the relics of human yearning towards the immense, the sight of which teases our mind out of thought. Does it not prove that in the

vision of a great Roman Empire the creative imagination of the
people rejoiced in the revelation of its transcendental humanity?
It was the idea of an Empire which was not merely for opening
an outlet to the pent-up pressure of over-population, or widening its field of commercial profit, but which existed as a concrete
representation of the majesty of Roman personality, the soul of
the people dreaming of a world-wide creation of its own for a
fit habitation of the Ideal Man. It was Rome's titanic endeavour
to answer the eternal question as to what Man truly was, as
Man. And any answer given in earnest falls within the realm of
religion, whatever may be its character; and this answer, in its
truth, belongs not only to any particular people but to us all. It
may be that Rome did not give the most perfect answer possible
when she fought for her place as a world-builder of human history, but she revealed the marvellous vigour of the indomitable
human spirit which could say, "*Bhumaiva sukham*", "Greatness
is happiness itself". Her Empire has been sundered and shattered, but her faith in the sublimity of man still persists in one
of the vast strata of human geology. And this faith was the true
spirit of her religion, which had been dim in the tradition of
her formal theology, merely supplying her with an emotional
pastime and not with spiritual inspiration. In fact this theology
fell far below her personality, and for that reason it went against
her religion, whose mission was to reveal her humanity on the
background of the eternal. Let us seek the religion of this and
other people not in their gods but in Man, who dreamed of his
own infinity and majestically worked for all time, defying danger and death.

Since the dim nebula of consciousness in Life's world became
intensified into a centre of self in Man, his history began to
unfold its rapid chapters; for it is the history of his strenuous

answers in various forms to the question rising from this conscious self of his, "What am I?" Man is not happy or contented as the animals are; for his happiness and his peace depend upon the truth of his answer. The animal attains his success in a physical sufficiency that satisfies his nature. When a crocodile finds no obstruction in behaving like an orthodox crocodile he grins and grows and has no cause to complain. It is truism to say that Man also must behave like a man in order to find his truth. But he is sorely puzzled and asks in bewilderment: "What is it to be like a man? What am I?" It is not left to the tiger to discover what is his own nature as a tiger, nor, for the matter of that, to choose a special colour for his coat according to his taste.

But Man has taken centuries to discuss the question of his own true nature and has not yet come to a conclusion. He has been building up elaborate religions to convince himself, against his natural inclinations, of the paradox that he is not what he is but something greater. What is significant about these efforts is the fact that in order to know himself truly Man in his religion cultivates the vision of a Being who exceeds him in truth and with whom also he has his kinship. These religions differ in details and often in their moral significance, but they have a common tendency. In them men seek their own supreme value, which they call divine, in some personality anthropomorphic in character. The mind, which is abnormally scientific, scoffs at this; but it should know that religion is not essentially cosmic or even abstract; it finds itself when it touches the Brahma in man; otherwise it has no justification to exist.

It must be admitted that such a human element introduces into our religion a mentality that often has its danger in aberrations that are intellectually blind, morally reprehensible and aesthetically repellent. But these are wrong answers; they distort the truth of man and, like all mistakes in sociology, in economics or politics, they have to be fought against and overcome. Their truth has to be judged by the standard of human perfection and not by some arbitrary injunction that refuses to be confirmed by the tribunal of the human conscience. And great religions are the outcome of great revolutions in this direction causing fundamental changes of our attitude. These religions invariably made their appearance as a protest against the earlier creeds which had been unhuman, where ritualistic observances had become more important and outer compulsions more imperious. These creeds were, as I have said before, cults of power; they had their value for us, not helping us to become perfect through truth, but to grow formidable through possessions and magic control of the deity.

But possibly I am doing injustice to our ancestors. It is more likely that they worshipped power not merely because of its utility, but because they, in their way, recognized it as truth with which their own power had its communication and in which it found its fulfilment. They must have naturally felt that this power was the power of will behind nature, and not some impersonal insanity that unaccountably always stumbled upon correct results. For it would have been the greatest depth of imbecility on their part had they brought their homage to an abstraction, mindless, heartless and purposeless; in fact, infinitely below them in its manifestation.

Chapter IV

Spiritual Union

WHEN Man's preoccupation with the means of livelihood became less insistent he had the leisure to come to the mystery of his own self, and could not help feeling that the truth of his personality had both its relationship and its perfection in an endless world of humanity. His religion, which in the beginning had its cosmic background of power, came to a higher stage when it found its background in the human truth of personality. It must not be thought that in this channel it was narrowing the range of our consciousness of the infinite.

The negative idea of the infinite is merely an indefinite enlargement of the limits of things; in fact, a perpetual postponement of infinitude. I am told that mathematics has come to the conclusion that our world belongs to a space which is limited. It does not make us feel disconsolate. We do not miss very much and need not have a low opinion of space even if a straight line cannot remain straight and has an eternal tendency to come back to the point from which it started. In the Hindu

Scripture the universe is described as an egg; that is to say, for the human mind it has its circular shell of limitation. The Hindu Scripture goes still further and says that time also is not continuous and our world repeatedly comes to an end to begin its cycle once again. In other words, in the region of time and space infinity consists of ever-revolving finitude.

But the positive aspect of the infinite is in *advaitam*, in an absolute unity, in which comprehension of the multitude is not as in an outer receptacle but as in an inner perfection that permeates and exceeds its contents, like the beauty in a lotus which is ineffably more than all the constituents of the flower. It is not the magnitude of extension but an intense quality of harmony which evokes in us the positive sense of the infinite in our joy, in our love. For *advaitam* is *anandam*; the infinite One is infinite Love. For those among whom the spiritual sense is dull, the desire for realization is reduced to physical possession, an actual grasping in space. This longing for magnitude becomes not an aspiration towards the great, but a mania for the big. But true spiritual realization is not through augmentation of possession in dimension or number. The truth that is infinite dwells in the ideal of unity which we find in the deeper relatedness. This truth of realization is not in space, it can only be realized in one's own inner spirit.

Ekadhaivanudrashtavyam etat aprameyam dhruvam.

(This infinite and eternal has to be known as One.)

Para akasat aja atma, "This birthless spirit is beyond space". For it is *Purushah*, it is the "Person".

The special mental attitude which India has in her religion is made clear by the word *Yoga*, whose meaning is to effect union.

Union has its significance not in the realm of *to have*, but in that of *to be*. To *gain* truth is to admit its separateness, but to *be* true is to become one with truth. Some religions, which deal with our relationship with God, assure us of reward if that relationship be kept true. This reward has an objective value. It gives us some reason outside ourselves for pursuing the prescribed path. We have such religions also in India. But those that have attained a greater height aspire for their fulfilment in union with *Narayana*, the supreme Reality of Man, which is divine.

Our union with this spirit is not to be attained through the mind. For our mind belongs to the department of economy in the human organism. It carefully husbands our consciousness for its own range of reason, within which to permit our relationship with the phenomenal world. But it is the object of *Yoga* to help us to transcend the limits built up by Mind. On the occasions when these are overcome, our inner self is filled with joy, which indicates that through such freedom we come into touch with the Reality that is an end in itself and therefore is bliss.

Once man had his vision of the infinite in the universal Light, and he offered his worship to the sun. He also offered his service to the fire with oblations. Then he felt the infinite in Life, which is Time in its creative aspect, and he said, "*Yat kincha yadidam sarvam prana ejati nihsritam*", "All that there is comes out of life and vibrates in it." He was sure of it, being conscious of Life's mystery immediately in himself as the principle of purpose, as the organized will, the source of all his activities. His interpretation of the ultimate character of truth relied upon the suggestion that Life had brought to him, and not the non-living which is dumb. And then he came deeper into his being and said, "*Raso vai sah*", "The infinite is love itself"—the eternal spirit of joy. His religion, which is in his realization of the infinite, began its journey from the impersonal *dyaus*, "the sky", wherein light had its manifestation; then came to Life, which represented the force of self-creation in time; and ended in *purushah*, the "Person", in whom dwells timeless love. It said, "*Tam vedyam purusham vedah*", "Know him the Person who is to be realized"; "*Yatha ma vo mrityuh parivyathah*", "So that death may not cause you sorrow." For this Person is deathless in whom the individual person has his immortal truth. Of him it is said: "*Esha devo visvakarma mahatma sada jananam hridaye sanni-vishatah*", "This is the divine being, the world-worker, who is the Great Soul ever dwelling inherent in the hearts of all people".

Ya etad vidur amritas te bhavanti, "Those who realize him, transcend the limits of mortality"—not in duration of time, but in perfection of truth.

Our union with a Being whose activity is world-wide and who dwells in the heart of humanity cannot be a passive one. In order to be united with Him we have to divest our work of selfishness and become *visvakarma*, "the world-worker", we must work for all. When I use the words "for all", I do not mean for a countless number of individuals. All work that is good, however small in extent, is universal in character. Such work makes for a realization of *Visvakarma*, "the World-Worker" who works for all. In order to be one with this Mahatma, "the Great Soul", one must cultivate the greatness of soul which identifies itself with the soul of all peoples and not merely with that of one's own. This helps us to understand what Buddha has described as *Brahmavihara*, "living in the infinite". He says:

"Do not deceive each other, do not despise anybody anywhere, never in anger wish anyone to suffer through your body, words or thoughts. Like a mother maintaining her only son with her own life, keep thy immeasurable loving thought for all creatures.

"Above thee, below thee, on all sides of thee, keep on all the world thy sympathy and immeasurable loving thought which is without obstruction, without any wish to injure, without enmity.

"To be dwelling in such contemplation while standing, walking, sitting or lying down, until sleep overcomes thee, is called living in Brahma."

This proves that Buddha's idea of the infinite was not the idea of a spirit of an unbounded cosmic activity, but the infinite whose meaning is in the positive ideal of goodness and love, which cannot be otherwise than human. By being charitable, good and loving, you do not realize the infinite in the stars or rocks, but the infinite revealed in Man. Buddha's teaching speaks of Nirvana as the highest end. To understand its real character we have to know the path of its attainment, which is not merely through the negation of evil thoughts and deeds but through the elimination of all limits to love. It must mean the sublimation of self in a truth which is love itself, which unites in its bosom all those to whom we must offer our sympathy and service.

When somebody asked Buddha about the original cause of existence he sternly said that such questioning was futile and irrelevant. Did he not mean that it went beyond the human sphere as our goal—that though such a question might legitimately be asked in the region of cosmic philosophy or science, it had nothing to do with man's *dharma*, man's inner nature, in which love finds its utter fulfilment, in which all his sacrifice ends in an eternal gain, in which the putting out of the lamplight is no loss because there is the all-pervading light of the sun? And did those who listened to the great teacher merely hear his words and understand his doctrines? No, they directly felt in him what he was preaching, in the living language of his own person, the ultimate truth of Man.

It is significant that all great religions have their historic origin in persons who represented in their life a truth which was not cosmic and unmoral, but human and good. They rescued religion from the magic stronghold of demon force and brought it into the inner heart of humanity, into a fulfilment not confined to some exclusive good fortune of the individual but to the welfare of all men. This was not for the spiritual ecstasy of lonely souls, but for the spiritual emancipation of all races. They came as the messengers of Man to men of all countries and spoke of the salvation that could only be reached by the perfecting of our relationship with Man the Eternal, Man the Divine. Whatever might be their doctrines of God, or some dogmas that they borrowed from their own time and tradition, their life and teaching had the deeper implication of a Being who is the infinite in Man, the Father, the Friend, the Lover, whose service must be realized through serving all mankind. For the God in Man depends upon men's service and men's love for his own love's fulfilment.

The question was once asked in the shade of the ancient forest of India:

Kasmai devaya havisha vidhema?

"Who is the God to whom we must bring our oblation?"

That question is still ours, and to answer it we must know in the depth of our love and the maturity of our wisdom what man is—know him not only in sympathy but in science, in the joy of creation and in the pain of heroism; *tena tyaktena bhunjitha,* "enjoy him through sacrifice"—the sacrifice that comes of love; *ma gridhah*, "covet not", for greed diverts your mind to that illusion in you which is your separate self and diverts it from truth in which you represent the *parama purushah*, "the supreme Person".

Our greed diverts our consciousness to materials away from that supreme value of truth which is the quality of the universal being. The gulf thus created by the receding stream of the soul we try to replenish with a continuous stream of wealth, which may have the power to fill but not the power to unite and recreate. Therefore the gap is dangerously concealed under the glittering quicksand of things, which by their own weight cause a sudden subsidence while we are in the depths of sleep.

The real tragedy, however, does not lie in the risk of our material security but in the obscuration of Man himself in the human world. In the creative activities of his soul Man realizes his surroundings as his larger self, instinct with his own life and love. But in his ambition he deforms and defiles it with the callous handling of his voracity. His world of utility, assuming a gigantic proportion, reacts upon his inner nature and hypnotically suggests to him a scheme of the universe which is an abstract system. In such a world there can be no question of *mukti*, the freedom in truth, because it is a solidly solitary fact, a cage with no sky beyond it. In all appearance our world is a closed world of hard facts; it is like a seed with its tough cover. But within this enclosure is working our silent cry of life for *mukti*, even when its possibility is darkly silent. When some huge overgrown temptation tramples into stillness this living aspiration then does civilization die like a seed that has lost its urging for germination. And this *mukti* is in the truth that dwells in the ideal man.

Chapter V

The Prophet

IN my introduction I have stated that the universe to which we are related through our sense perception, reason or imagination, is necessarily Man's universe. Our physical self gains strength and success through its correct relationship in knowledge and practice with its physical aspect. The mysteries of all its phenomena are generalized by man as laws which have their harmony with his rational mind. In the primitive period of our history Man's physical dealings with the external world were most important for the maintenance of his life, the life which he has in common with other creatures, and therefore the first expression of his religion was physical—it came from his sense of wonder and awe at the manifestations of power in Nature and his attempt to win it for himself and his tribe by magical incantations and rites. In other words his religion tried to gain a perfect communion with the mysterious magic of Nature's forces through his own power of magic. Then came the time when he had the freedom of leisure to divert his mind to his inner nature and the mystery of his own personality gained for him its highest importance. And instinctively his personal self sought its fulfilment in the truth of a higher personality. In the history of religion our realization of its nature has gone through many changes even like our realization of the nature of the material world. Our method of worship has followed the course of such changes, but its evolution has been from the external and magical towards the moral and spiritual significance.

The first profound record of the change of direction in Man's religion we find in the message of the great prophet in Persia, Zarathustra, and as usual it was accompanied by a revolution. In a later period the same thing happened in India, and it is evident that the history of this religious struggle lies embedded in the epic Mahabharata associated with the name of Krishna and the teachings of Bhagavadgita.

The most important of all outstanding facts of Iranian history is the religious reform brought about by Zarathustra. There can be hardly any question that he was the first man we know who gave a definitely moral character and direction to religion and at the same time preached the doctrine of monotheism which offered an eternal foundation of reality to goodness as an ideal of perfection. All religions of the primitive type try to keep men bound with regulations of external observances. Zarathustra was the greatest of all the pioneer prophets who showed the path of freedom to man, the freedom of moral choice, the freedom from the blind obedience to unmeaning injunctions, the freedom from the multiplicity of shrines which draw our worship away from the single-minded chastity of devotion.

To most of us it sounds like a truism to-day when we are told that the moral goodness of a deed comes from the goodness of intention. But it is a truth which once came to Man like a revelation of light in the darkness and it has not yet reached all the obscure corners of humanity. We still see around us men who fearfully follow, hoping thereby to gain merit, the path of blind formalism, which has no living moral source in the mind. This will make us understand the greatness of Zarathustra. Though surrounded by believers in magical rites, he proclaimed in those dark days of unreason that religion has its truth in its moral significance, not in external practices of imaginary value; that its value is in upholding man in his life of good thoughts, good words and good deeds.

"The prophet", says Dr. Geiger, "qualifies his religion as 'unheard of words' (Yasna 31. 1) or as a 'mystery' (Y. 48. 3.) because he himself regards it as a religion quite distinct from the belief of the people hitherto. The revelation he announces is to him no longer a matter of sentiment, no longer a merely undefined presentiment and conception of the Godhead, but a matter of intellect, of spiritual perception and knowledge. This is of great importance, for there are probably not many religions of so high antiquity in which this fundamental doctrine, that religion is a knowledge or learning, a science of what is true, is so precisely declared as in the tenets of the Gathas. It is the unbelieving that are unknowing; on the contrary, the believing are learned because they have penetrated into this knowledge."

It may be incidentally mentioned here, as showing the parallel to this in the development of Indian religious thought, that all through the Upanishad spiritual truth is termed with a repeated emphasis, *vidya*, knowledge, which has for its opposite *avidya*, acceptance of error born of unreason.

The outer expression of truth reaches its white light of simplicity through its inner realization. True simplicity is the physiognomy of perfection. In the primitive stages of spiritual growth, when man is dimly aware of the mystery of the infinite in his life and the world, when he does not fully know the inward character of his relationship with this truth, his first feeling is either of dread, or of greed of gain. This drives him into wild exaggeration in worship, frenzied convulsions of ceremonialism. But in Zarathustra's teachings, which are best reflected in his Gathas, we have hardly any mention of the ritualism of worship. Conduct and its moral motives have there received almost the sole attention.

The orthodox Persian form of worship in ancient Iran included animal sacrifices and offering of *haema* to the *daevas*. That all these should be discountenanced by Zarathustra not only shows his courage, but the strength of his realization of the Supreme Being as spirit. We are told that it has been mentioned by Plutarch that "Zarathustra taught the Persians to sacrifice to Ahura Mazda, 'vows and thanksgivings'". The distance between faith in the efficiency of the blood-stained magical rites and cultivation of the moral and spiritual ideals as the true form of worship is immense. It is amazing to see how Zarathustra was the first among men who crossed this distance with a certainty of realization which imparted such a fervour of faith to his life and his words. The truth which filled his mind was not a thing which he borrowed from books or received from teachers; he did not come to it by following a prescribed path of tradition, but it came to him as an illumination of his entire life, almost like a communication of his universal self to his personal self, and he proclaimed this utmost immediacy of his knowledge when he said:

> When I conceived of Thee, O Mazda, as the very
> First and the Last, as the most Adorable One, as
> the Father of the Good Thought, as the Creator of
> Truth and Right, as the Lord Judge of our actions
> in life, then I made a place for Thee in my very eyes.
> —Yasna 31.8 (Translation D. J. Irani).

It was the direct stirring of his soul which made him say:

> Thus do I announce the Greatest of all! I weave
> my songs of praise for him through Truth, helpful
> and beneficent of all that live. Let Ahura Mazda
> listen to them with his Holy Spirit, for the Good
> Mind instructed me to adore Him; by his wisdom
> let Him teach me about what is best. —Yasna 45.6
> (Translation D. J. Irani).

The truth which is not reached through the analytical process of reasoning and does not depend for proof on some corroboration of outward facts or the prevalent faith and practice of the people—the truth which comes like an inspiration out of context with its surroundings brings with it an assurance that it has been sent from an inner source of divine wisdom, that the individual who has realized it is specially inspired and therefore has his responsibility as a direct medium of communication of Divine Truth.

As long as man deals with his God as the dispenser of benefits only to those of His worshippers who know the secret of propitiating Him, he tries to keep Him for his own self or for the tribe to which he belongs. But directly the moral nature, that is to say, the humanity of God is apprehended, man realizes his divine self in his religion, his God is no longer an outsider to be propitiated for a special concession. The consciousness of God transcends the limitations of race and gathers together all human beings within one spiritual circle of union. Zarathustra was the first prophet who emancipated religion from the exclusive narrowness of the tribal God, the God of a chosen people, and offered it the universal Man. This is a great fact in the history of religion. The Master said, when the enlightenment came to him:

> Verily I believed Thee, O Ahura Mazda, to be the Supreme Benevolent Providence, when Sraosha came to me with the Good Mind, when first I received and became wise with your words. And though the task be difficult, though woe may come to me, I shall proclaim to all mankind Thy message, which Thou declarest to be the best. —Yasna 43 (Translation D. J. Irani).

He prays to Mazda:

> This I ask Thee, tell me truly, O Ahura, the religion that is best for all mankind, the religion, which based on truth, should prosper in all that is ours, the religion which establishes our actions in order and justice by the Divine songs of Perfect Piety, which has for its intelligent desire of desires, the desire for Thee, O Mazda. —Yasna 44.10 (Translation D. J. Irani).

With the undoubted assurance and hope of one who has got a direct vision of Truth he speaks to the world:

Hearken unto me, Ye who come from near and from far! Listen for I shall speak forth now; ponder well over all things, weigh my words with care and clear thought. Never shall the false teacher destroy this world for a second time, for his tongue stands mute, his creed exposed. —Yasna 45.1 (Translation D. J. Irani).

I think it can be said without doubt that such a high conception of religion, uttered in such a clear note of affirmation with a sure note of conviction that it is a truth of the ultimate ideal of perfection which must be revealed to all humanity, even at the cost of martyrdom, is unique in the history of any religion belonging to such a remote dawn of civilization.

There was a time when, along with other Aryan peoples, the Persian also worshipped the elemental gods of Nature, whose favour was not to be won by any moral duty performed or service of love. That in fact was the crude beginning of the scientific spirit trying to unlock the hidden sources of power in nature. But through it all there must have been some current of deeper desire, which constantly contradicted the cult of power and indicated worlds of inner good, infinitely more precious than material gain. Its voice was not strong at first nor was it heeded by the majority of the people; but its influences, like the life within the seed, were silently working.

Then comes the great prophet; and in his life and mind the hidden fire of truth suddenly bursts out into flame. The best in the people works for long obscure ages in hints and whispers till it finds its voice which can never again be silenced. For that voice becomes the voice of Man, no longer confined to a particular time or people. It works across intervals of silence and oblivion, depression and defeat, and comes out again with its conquering call. It is a call to the fighter, the fighter against untruth, against all that lures away man's spirit from its high mission of freedom into the meshes of materialism.

Zarathustra's voice is still a living voice, not alone a matter of academic interest for historical scholars who deal with the facts of the past; nor merely the guide of a small community of men in the daily details of their life. Rather, of all teachers Zarathustra was the first who addressed his words to all humanity, regardless of distance of space or time. He was not like a cavedweller who, by some chance of friction, had lighted a lamp and, fearing lest it could not be shared with all, secured it with a miser's care for his own domestic use. But he was the watcher in the night, who stood on the lonely peak facing the East and broke out singing the paeans of light to the sleeping world when the sun came out on the brim of the horizon. The Sun of Truth is for all, he declared—its light is to unite the far and the near. Such a message always arouses the antagonism of those whose habits have become nocturnal, whose vested interest is in the darkness. And there was a bitter fight in the lifetime of the prophet between his followers and the other who were addicted to the ceremonies that had tradition on their side, and not truth.

We are told that "Zarathustra was descended from a kingly family", and also that the first converts to his doctrine were of the ruling caste. But the priesthood, "the Kavis and the Karapans, often succeeded in bringing the rulers over to their side". So we find that, in this fight, the princes of the land divided themselves into two opposite parties, as we find in India in the Kurukshetra War.

It has been a matter of supreme satisfaction to me to realize that the purification of faith which was the mission of the great teachers in both communities, in Persia and in India, followed a similar line. We have already seen how Zarathustra spiritualized the meaning of sacrifice, which in former days consisted in external ritualism entailing bloodshed. The same thing we find in the Gita, in which the meaning of the word *Yajna* has been translated into a higher significance than it had in its crude form.

According to the Gita, the deeds that are done solely for the sake of self fetter our soul; the disinterested action, performed for the sake of the giving up of self, is the true sacrifice. For creation itself comes of the self-sacrifice of Brahma, which has no other purpose; and therefore, in our performance of the duty which is self-sacrificing, we realize the spirit of Brahma.

The ideal of Zoroastrian Persia is distinctly ethical. It sends its call to men to work together with the Eternal Spirit of Good in spreading and maintaining *Kshathra*, the kingdom of righteousness, against all attacks of evil. This ideal gives us our place as collaborators with God in distributing his blessings over the world.

> Clear is this to the man of wisdom as to the man
>   who carefully thinks;
> He who upholds Truth with all the might of his
>   power,
> He who upholds Truth the utmost in his words and
>   deed,
> He, indeed, is Thy most valued helper, O Mazda
>   Ahura! —Yasna 31.22 (Translation D. J. Irani).

It is a fact of supreme moment to us that the human world is in an incessant state of war between that which will save us and that which will drag us into the abyss of disaster. Our one hope lies in the fact that Ahura Mazda is on our side if we choose the right course.

The active heroic aspect of this religion reflects the character of the people themselves, who later on spread conquests far and wide and built up great empires by the might of their sword. They accepted this world in all seriousness. They had their zest in life and confidence in their own strength. They belonged to the western half of Asia and their great influence travelled through the neighbouring civilization of Judaea towards the Western Continent. Their ideal was the ideal of the fighter. By force of will and deeds of sacrifice they were to conquer *haurvatat*—welfare in this world, and *ameratat*—immortality in the other. This is the best ideal in the West, the great truth of fight. For paradise has to be gained through conquest. That sacred task is for the heroes, who are to take the right side in the battle, and the right weapons.

There was a heroic period in Indian history, when this holy spirit of fight was invoked by the greatest poet of the Sanskrit literature. It is not to be wondered at that his ideal of fight was similar to the ideal that Zarathustra preached. The problem with which his poem starts is that paradise has to be rescued by the hero from its invasion by evil beings. This is the eternal problem of man. The evil spirit is exultant and paradise is lost when *Sati*, the spirit of *Sat* (Reality), is disunited from *Siva*, the Spirit of Goodness. The Real and the Good must meet in wedlock if the hero is to take his birth in order to save all that is true and beautiful. When the union was attempted through the agency of passion, the anger of God was aroused and the result was a tragedy of disappointment. At last, by purification through penance, the wedding was effected, the hero was born who fought against the forces of evil and paradise was regained. This is a poem of the ideal of the moral fight, whose first great prophet was Zarathustra.

We must admit that this ideal has taken a stronger hold upon the life of man in the West than in India—the West, where the vigour of life receives its fullest support from Nature and the excess of energy finds its delight in ceaseless activities. But everywhere in the world, the unrealized ideal is a force of disaster. It gathers its strength in secret even in the heart of prosperity, kills the soul first and then drives men to their utter ruin. When the aggressive activity of will, which naturally accompanies physical vigour, fails to accept the responsibility of its ideal, it breeds unappeasable greed for material gain, leads to unmeaning slavery of things, till amidst a raging conflagration of clashing interests the tower of ambition topples down to the dust.

And for this, the prophetic voice of Zarathustra reminds us that all human activities must have an ideal goal, which is an end to itself, and therefore is peace, is immortality. It is the House of Songs, the realization of love, which comes through strenuous service of goodness.

> All the joys of life which Thou holdest, O Mazda,
> the joys that were, the joys that are, and the joys that
> shall be, Thou dost apportion all in Thy love for us.

We, on the other hand, in the tropical East, who have no surplus of physical energy inevitably overflowing in outer activities, also have our own ideal given to us. Our course is not so much through the constant readiness to fight in the battle of the good and evil, as through the inner concentration of mind, through pacifying the turbulence of desire, to reach that serenity of the infinite in our being which leads to the harmony in the all. Here, likewise, the unrealized ideal pursues us with its malediction. As the activities of a vigorous vitality may become unmeaning, and thereupon smother the soul with a mere multiplicity of material, so the peace of the extinguished desire may become the peace of death; and the inner world, in which we would dwell, become a world of incoherent dreams.

The negative process of curbing desire and controlling passion is only for saving our energy from dissipation and directing it into its proper channel. If the path of the channel we have chosen runs withinwards, it also must have its expression in action, not for any ulterior reward, but for the proving of its own truth. If the test of action is removed, if our realization grows purely subjective, then it may become like travelling in a desert in the night, going round and round the same circle, imagining all the while that we are following the straight path of purpose.

This is why the prophet of the Gita in the first place says:

> Whoso forsakes all desires and goeth onwards free
> from yearnings, selfless and without egoism, he
> goeth to peace.

But he does not stop here, he adds:

> Surrendering all actions to me, with Thy thoughts
> resting on the Supreme Self, from hope and egoism
> freed, and of mental fever cured, engage in battle.

Action there must be, fight we must have—not the fight of passion and desire, or arrogant self-assertion, but of duty done in the presence of the Eternal, the disinterested fight of the serene soul that helps us in our union with the Supreme Being.

In this, the teaching of Zarathustra, his sacred gospel of fight finds its unity. The end of the fight he preaches is in the House of Songs, in the symphony of spiritual union. He sings:

> Ye, who wish to be allied to the Good Mind, to be friend with Truth, Ye who desire to sustain the Holy Cause, down with all anger and violence, away with all ill-will and strife! Such benevolent men, O Mazda, I shall take to the House of Songs!

The detailed facts of history, which are the battleground of the learned, are not my province. I am a singer myself, and I am ever attracted by the strains that come forth from the House of Songs. When the streams of ideals that flow from the East and from the West mingle their murmur in some profound harmony of meaning it delights my soul.

In the realm of material property men are jealously proud of their possessions and their exclusive rights. Unfortunately there are quarrelsome men who bring that pride of acquisition, the worldliness of sectarianism, even into the region of spiritual truth. Would it be sane, if the man in China should lay claim to the ownership of the sun because he can prove the earlier sunrise in his own country?

For myself, I feel proud whenever I find that the best in the world have their fundamental agreement. It is their function to unite and to dissuade the small from bristling-up, like prickly shrubs, in the pride of the minute points of their differences, only to hurt one another.

Chapter VI

The Vision

I hope that my readers have understood, as they have read these pages, that I am neither a scholar nor a philosopher. They should not expect from me fruits gathered from a wide field of studies or wealth brought by a mind trained in the difficult exploration of knowledge. Fortunately for me the subject of religion gains in interest and value by the experience of the individuals who earnestly believe in its truth. This is my apology for offering a part of the story of my life which has always realized its religion through a process of growth and not by the help of inheritance or importation.

Man has made the entire geography of the earth his own, ignoring the boundaries of climate; for, unlike the lion and the reindeer, he has the power to create his special skin and temperature, including his unscrupulous power of borrowing the skins of the indigenous inhabitants and misappropriating their fats.

His kingdom is also continually extending in time through

a great surplus in his power of memory, to which is linked his immense facility of borrowing the treasure of the past from all quarters of the world. He dwells in a universe of history, in an environment of continuous remembrance. The animal occupies time only through the multiplication of its own race, but man through the memorials of his mind, raised along the pilgrimage of progress. The stupendousness of his knowledge and wisdom is due to their roots spreading into and drawing sap from the far-reaching area of history.

Man has his other dwelling-place in the realm of inner realization, in the element of an immaterial value. This is a world where from the subterranean soil of his mind his consciousness often, like a seed, unexpectedly sends up sprouts into the heart of a luminous freedom, and the individual is made to realize his truth in the universal Man. I hope it may prove of interest if I give an account of my own personal experience of a sudden spiritual outburst from within me which is like the underground current of a perennial stream unexpectedly welling up on the surface.

I was born in a family which, at that time, was earnestly developing a monotheistic religion based upon the philosophy of the Upanishad. Somehow my mind at first remained coldly aloof, absolutely uninfluenced by any religion whatever. It was through an idiosyncrasy of my temperament that I refused to accept any religious teaching merely because people in my surroundings believed it to be true. I could not persuade myself to imagine that I had a religion because everybody whom I might trust believed in its value.

Thus my mind was brought up in an atmosphere of freedom—freedom from the dominance of any creed that had its sanction in the definite authority of some scripture, or in the teaching of some organized body of worshippers. And, there-fore, the man who questions me has every right to distrust my vision and reject my testimony. In such a case, the authority of some particular book venerated by a large number of men may have greater weight than the assertion of an individual, and therefore I never claim any right to preach.

When I look back upon those days, it seems to me that unconsciously I followed the path of my Vedic ancestors, and was inspired by the tropical sky with its suggestion of an utter-most Beyond. The wonder of the gathering clouds hanging heavy with the unshed rain, of the sudden sweep of storms arousing vehement gestures along the line of coconut trees, the fierce loneliness of the blazing summer noon, the silent sunrise be-hind the dewy veil of autumn morning, kept my mind with the intimacy of a pervasive companionship.

Then came my initiation ceremony of Brahminhood when the *gayatri* verse of meditation was given to me, whose meaning, according to the explanation I had, runs as follows:

> Let me contemplate the adorable splendour of Him
> who created the earth, the air and the starry spheres,
> and sends the power of comprehension within our
> minds.

This produced a sense of serene exaltation in me, the daily med-itation upon the infinite being which unites in one stream of creation my mind and the outer world. Though to-day I find no difficulty in realizing this being as an infinite personality in whom the subject and object are perfectly reconciled, at that time the idea to me was vague. Therefore the current of feeling that it aroused in my mind was indefinite, like the circulation of air—an atmosphere which needed a definite world to complete itself and satisfy me. For it is evident that my religion is a poet's religion, and neither that of an orthodox man of piety nor that of a theologian. Its touch comes to me through the same unseen and trackless channel as does the inspiration of my songs. My religious life has followed the same mysterious line of growth as has my poetical life. Somehow they are wedded to each other and, though their betrothal had a long period of ceremony, it was kept secret to me

When I was eighteen, a sudden spring breeze of religious experience for the first time came to my life and passed away leaving in my memory a direct message of spiritual reality. One day while I stood watching at early dawn the sun sending out its rays from behind the trees, I suddenly felt as if some ancient mist had in a moment lifted from my sight, and the morning light on the face of the world revealed an inner radiance of joy. The invisible screen of the commonplace was removed from all things and all men, and their ultimate significance was intensified in my mind; and this is the definition of beauty. That which was memorable in this experience was its human message, the sudden expansion of my consciousness in the super-personal world of man. The poem I wrote on the first day of my surprise was named "The Awakening of the Waterfall". The waterfall, whose spirit lay dormant in its ice-bound isolation, was touched by the sun and, bursting in a cataract of freedom, it found its finality in an unending sacrifice, in a continual union with the sea. After four days the vision passed away, and the lid hung down upon my inner sight. In the dark, the world once again put on its disguise of the obscurity of an ordinary fact.

When I grew older and was employed in a responsible work in some villages I took my place in a neighbourhood where the current of time ran slow and joys and sorrows had their simple and elemental shades and lights. The day which had its special significance for me came with all its drifting trivialities of the commonplace life. The ordinary work of my morning had come to its close, and before going to take my bath I stood for a moment at my window, overlooking a marketplace on the bank of a dry river bed, welcoming the first flood of rain along its channel. Suddenly I became conscious of a stirring of soul within me. My world of experience in a moment seemed to become lighted, and facts that were detached and dim found a great unity of meaning. The feeling which I had was like that which a man, groping through a fog without knowing his destination, might feel when he suddenly discovers that he stands before his own house.

I still remember the day in my childhood when I was made to struggle across my lessons in a first primer, strewn with isolated words smothered under the burden of spelling. The morning hour appeared to me like a once-illumined page, grown dusty and faded, discoloured into irrelevant marks, smudges and gaps, wearisome in its moth-eaten meaninglessness. Suddenly I came to a rhymed sentence of combined words, which may be translated thus— "It rains, the leaves tremble". At once I came to a world wherein I recovered my full meaning. My mind touched the creative realm of expression, and at that moment I was no longer a mere student with his mind muffled by spelling lessons, enclosed by classroom. The rhythmic picture of the tremulous leaves beaten by the rain opened before my mind the world which does not merely carry information, but a harmony with my being. The unmeaning fragments lost their individual isolation and my mind revelled in the unity of a vision. In a similar manner, on that morning in the village the facts of my life suddenly appeared to me in a luminous unity of truth. All things that had seemed like vagrant waves were revealed to my mind in relation to a boundless sea. I felt sure that some Being who comprehended me and my world was seeking his best expression in all my experiences, uniting them into an ever-widening individuality which is a spiritual work of art.

To this Being I was responsible; for the creation in me is his as well as mine. It may be that it was the same creative Mind that is shaping the universe to its eternal idea; but in me as a person it had one of its special centres of a personal relationship growing into a deepening consciousness. I had my sorrows that left their memory in a long burning track across my days, but I felt at that moment that in them I lent myself to a travail of creation that ever exceeded my own personal bounds like stars which in their individual fire-bursts are lighting the history of the universe. It gave me a great joy to feel in my life detachment at the idea of a mystery of a meeting of the two in a creative comradeship. I felt that I had found my religion at last, the religion of Man, in which the infinite became defined in humanity and came close to me so as to need my love and co-operation.

This idea of mine found at a later date its expression in some of my poems addressed to what I called *Jivan devata*, the Lord of my life. Fully aware of my awkwardness in dealing with a foreign language, with some hesitation I give a translation, being sure that any evidence revealed through the self-recording instrument of poetry is more authentic than answers extorted through conscious questionings

> Thou who art the innermost Spirit of my being,
> art thou pleased,
> > Lord of my Life?
> For I gave to thee my cup

filled with all the pain and delight
that the crushed grapes of my heart had surrendered,
I wove with the rhythm of colours and songs the cover
for thy bed,
and with the molten gold of my desires
I fashioned playthings for thy passing hours.

I know not why thou chosest me for thy partner,
     Lord of my life!
Didst thou store my days and nights,
my deeds and dreams for the alchemy of thy art,
and string in the chain of thy music my songs of autumn
     and spring,
and gather the flowers from my mature moments for thy
     crown?

I see thine eyes gazing at the dark of my heart,
     Lord of my Life,
I wonder if my failures and wrongs are forgiven.
For many were my days without service
and nights of forgetfulness;
futile were the flowers that faded in the shade not offered
     to thee.

Often the tired strings of my lute
slackened at the strain of thy tunes.
And often at the ruin of wasted hours
my desolate evenings were filled with tears.

But have my days come to their end at last,
     Lord of my life,

while my arms round thee grow limp,
my kisses losing their truth?
Then break up the meeting of this languid day.
Renew the old in me in fresh forms of delight;
and let the wedding come once again
in a new ceremony of life.

You will understand from this how unconsciously I had been travelling toward the realization which I stumbled upon in an idle moment on a day in July, when morning clouds thickened on the eastern horizon and a caressing shadow lay on the tremulous bamboo branches, while an excited group of village boys was noisily dragging from the bank an old fishing-boat; and I cannot tell how at that moment an unexpected train of thoughts ran across my mind like a strange caravan carrying the wealth of an unknown kingdom.

From my infancy I had a keen sensitiveness which kept my mind tingling with consciousness of the world around me, natural and human. We had a small garden attached to our house; it was a fairyland to me, where miracles of beauty were of everyday occurrence.

Almost every morning in the early hour of the dusk, I would run out from my bed in a great hurry to greet the first pink flush of the dawn through the shivering branches of the palm trees which stood in a line along the garden boundary, while the grass glistened as the dew-drops caught the earliest tremor of the morning breeze. The sky seemed to bring to me the call of a personal companionship, and all my heart—my whole body in fact—used to drink in at a draught the overflowing light and peace of those silent hours. I was anxious never to miss a single morning, because each one was precious to me, more precious than gold to the miser. I am certain that I felt a larger meaning of my own self when the barrier vanished between me and what was beyond myself.

I had been blessed with that sense of wonder which gives a child his right of entry into the treasure house of mystery in the depth of existence. My studies in the school I neglected, because they rudely dismembered me from the context of my world and I felt miserable, like a caged rabbit in a biological institute. This, perhaps, will explain the meaning of my religion. This world was living to me, intimately close to my life, permeated by a subtle touch of kinship which enhanced the value of my own being.

It is true that this world also has its impersonal aspect of truth which is pursued by the man of impersonal science. The father has his personal relationship with his son; but as a doctor he may detach the fact of a son from that relationship and let the child become an abstraction to him, only a living body with its physiological functions. It cannot be said that if through the constant pursuit of his vocations he altogether discards the personal element in his relation to his son he reaches a greater truth as a doctor than he does as a father. The scientific knowledge of his son is information about a fact, and not the realization of a truth. In his intimate feeling for his son he touches an ultimate truth—the truth of relationship, the truth of a harmony in the universe, the fundamental principle of creation. It is not merely the number of protons and electrons which represents the truth of an element; it is the mystery of their relationship which cannot be analysed. We are made conscious of this truth of relationship immediately within us in our love, in our joy; and from this experience of ours we have the right to say that the

Supreme One, who relates all things, comprehends the universe, is all love—the love that is the highest truth being the most perfect relationship.

I still remember the shock of repulsion I received as a child when some medical student brought to me a piece of a human windpipe and tried to excite my admiration for its structure. He tried to convince me that it was the source of the beautiful human voice. But I could not bear the artisan to occupy the throne that was for the artist who concealed the machinery and revealed the creation in its ineffable unity. God does not care to keep exposed the record of his power written in geological inscriptions, but he is proudly glad of the expression of beauty which he spreads on the green grass, in the flowers, in the play of the colours on the clouds, in the murmuring music of running water.

I had a vague notion as to who or what it was that touched my heart's chords, like the infant which does not know its mother's name, or who or what she is. The feeling which I always had was a deep satisfaction of personality that flowed into my nature through living channels of communication from all sides.

I am afraid that the scientist may remind me that to lose sight of the distinction between life and non-life, the human and the non-human, is a sign of the primitive mind. While admitting it, let me hope that it is not an utter condemnation, but rather the contrary. It may be a true instinct of Science itself, an instinctive logic, which makes the primitive mind think that humanity has become possible as a fact only because of a universal human truth which has harmony with its reason, with its will. In the details of our universe there are some differences that may be described as non-human, but not in their essence. The bones are different from the muscles, but they are organically one in the body. Our feeling of joy, our imagination, realizes a profound organic unity with the universe comprehended by the human mind. Without minimizing the differences that are in detailed manifestations, there is nothing wrong in trusting the mind, which is occasionally made intensely conscious of an all-pervading personality answering to the personality of man.

The details of reality must be studied in their differences by Science, but it can never know the character of the grand unity of relationship pervading it, which can only be realized immediately by the human spirit. And therefore it is the primal imagination of man—the imagination which is fresh and immediate in its experiences—that exclaims in a poet's verse:

> Wisdom and spirit of the universe!
> Thou soul, that art the eternity of thought,
> And giv'st to forms and images a breath
> And everlasting motion.

And in another poet's words it speaks of

> That light whose smile kindles the universe,
> That Beauty in which all things work and move.

The theologian may follow the scientist and shake his head and say that all that I have written is pantheism. But let us not indulge in an idolatry of name and dethrone living truth in its favour. When I say that I am a man, it is implied by that word that there is such a thing as a general idea of Man which persistently manifests itself in every particular human being, who is different from all other individuals. If we lazily label such a belief as "pananthropy" and divert our thoughts from its mysteriousness by such a title it does not help us much. Let me assert my faith by saying that this world, consisting of what we call animate and inanimate things, has found its culmination in man, its best expression. Man, as a creation, represents the Creator, and this is why of all creatures it has been possible for him to comprehend this world in his knowledge and in his feeling and in his imagination, to realize in his individual spirit a union with a Spirit that is everywhere.

There is an illustration that I have made use of in which I supposed that a stranger from some other planet has paid a visit to our earth and happens to hear the sound of a human voice on the gramophone. All that is obvious to him and most seemingly active, is the revolving disc. He is unable to discover the personal truth that lies behind, and so might accept the impersonal scientific fact of the disc as final—the fact that could be touched and measured. He would wonder how it could be possible for a machine to speak to the soul. Then, if in pursuing the mystery, he should suddenly come to the heart of the music through a meeting with the composer, he would at once understand the meaning of that music as a personal communication.

That which merely gives us information can be explained in terms of measurement, but that which gives us joy cannot be explained by the facts of a mere grouping of atoms and molecules. Somewhere in the arrangement of this world there seems to be a great concern about giving us delight, which shows that, in the universe, over and above the meaning of matter and forces, there is a message conveyed through the magic touch of personality. This touch cannot be analysed, it can only be felt. We cannot prove it any more than the man from the other planet could prove to the satisfaction of his fellows the personality which remained invisible, but which, through the machinery, spoke direct to the heart.

Is it merely because the rose is round and pink that it gives me more satisfaction than the gold which could buy me the necessities of life, or any number of slaves? One may, at the outset, deny the truth that a rose gives more delight than a piece of gold. But such an objector must remember that I am not speaking of artificial values. If we had to cross a desert whose sand was made of gold, then the cruel glitter of these dead particles would become a terror for us, and the sight of a rose would bring to us the music of paradise.

The final meaning of the delight which we find in a rose can never be in the roundness of its petals, just as the final meaning of the joy of music cannot be in a gramophone disc. Somehow we feel that through a rose the language of love reached our heart. Do we not carry a rose to our beloved because in it is already embodied a message which, unlike our language of words, cannot be analysed. Through this gift of a rose we utilize a universal language of joy for our own purposes of expression.

Fortunately for me a collection of old lyrical poems composed by the poets of the Vaishnava sect came to my hand when I was young. I became aware of some underlying idea deep in the obvious meaning of these love poems. I felt the joy of an explorer who suddenly discovers the key to the language lying hidden in the hieroglyphs which are beautiful in themselves. I was sure that these poets were speaking about the supreme Lover, whose touch we experience in all our relations of love—the love of nature's beauty, of the animal, the child, the comrade, the beloved, the love that illuminates our consciousness of reality. They sang of a love that ever flows through numerous obstacles between men and Man the Divine, the eternal relation which has the relationship of mutual dependence for a fulfilment that needs perfect union of individuals and the Universal.

The Vaishnava poet sings of the Lover who has his flute which, with its different stops, gives out the varied notes of beauty and love that are in Nature and Man. These notes bring to us our message of invitation. They eternally urge us to come out from the seclusion of our self-centred life into the realm of love and truth. Are we deaf by nature, or is it that we have been deafened by the claims of the world, of self-seeking, by the clamorous noise of the market-place? We miss the voice of the Lover, and we fight, we rob, we exploit the weak, we chuckle at our cleverness, when we can appropriate for our use what is due to others; we make our lives a desert by turning away from our world that stream of love which pours down from the blue sky and wells up from the bosom of the earth.

In the region of Nature, by unlocking the secret doors of the workshop department, one may come to that dark hall where dwells the mechanic and help to attain usefulness, but through it one can never attain finality. Here is the storehouse of innumerable facts and, however necessary they may be, they have not the treasure of fulfilment in them. But the hall of union is there, where dwells the Lover in the heart of existence. When a man reaches it he at once realizes that he has come to Truth, to immortality, and he is glad with a gladness which is an end, and yet which has no end.

Mere information about facts, mere discovery of power, belongs to the outside and not to the inner soul of things. Gladness is the one criterion of truth, and we know when we have touched Truth by the music it gives, by the joy of greeting it sends forth to the truth in us. That is the true foundation of all religions. It is not as ether waves that we receive light; the morning does not wait for some scientist for its introduction to us. In the same way we touch the infinite reality immediately within us only when we perceive the pure truth of love or goodness, not through the explanations of theologians, not through the erudite discussion of ethical doctrines.

I have already made the confession that my religion is a poet's religion. All that I feel about it is from vision and not from knowledge. Frankly, I acknowledge that I cannot satisfactorily answer any questions about evil, or about what happens after death. Nevertheless, I am sure that there have come moments in my own experience when my soul has touched the infinite and has become intensely conscious of it through the illumination of joy. It has been said in our Upanishad that our mind and our words come away baffled from the Supreme Truth, but he who knows truth through the immediate joy of his own soul is saved from all doubts and fears.

In the night we stumble over things and become acutely conscious of their individual separateness. But the day reveals the greater unity which embraces them. The man whose inner vision is bathed in an illumination of his consciousness at once realizes the spiritual unity reigning supreme over all differences. His mind no longer awkwardly stumbles over individual facts of separateness in the human world, accepting them as final. He realizes that peace is in the inner harmony which dwells in truth and not in any outer adjustments. He knows that beauty carries an eternal assurance of our spiritual relationship to reality, which waits for its perfection in the response of our love.

Chapter VII

The Man of My Heart

AT the outburst of an experience which is unusual, such as happened to me in the beginning of my youth, the puzzled mind seeks its explanation in some settled foundation of that which is usual, trying to adjust an unexpected inner message to an organized belief which goes by the general name of a religion. And, therefore, I naturally was glad at that time of youth to accept from my father the post of secretary to a special section of the monotheistic church of which he was the leader. I took part in its services mainly by composing hymns which unconsciously took the many-thumbed impression of the orthodox mind, a composite smudge of tradition. Urged by my sense of duty I strenuously persuaded myself to think that my new mental attitude was in harmony with that of the members of our association, although I constantly stumbled upon obstacles and felt constraints that hurt me to the quick.

At last I came to discover that in my conduct I was not strictly loyal to my religion, but only to the religious institution. This latter represented an artificial average, with its standard of truth at its static minimum, jealous of any vital growth that exceeded its limits. I have my conviction that in religion, and also in the arts, that which is common to a group is not important. Indeed, very often it is a contagion of mutual imitation. After a long struggle with the feeling that I was using a mask to hide the living face of truth, I gave up my connection with our church.

About this time, one day I chanced to hear a song from a beggar belonging to the Baül sect of Bengal. We have in the modern Indian Religion deities of different names, forms and mythology, some Vedic and other aboriginal. They have their special sectarian idioms and associations that give emotional satisfaction to those who are accustomed to their hypnotic influences. Some of them may have their aesthetic value to me and others philosophical significance overcumbered by exuberant distraction of legendary myths. But what struck me in this simple song was a religious expression that was neither grossly concrete, full of crude details, nor metaphysical in its rarified transcendentalism. At the same time it was alive with an emotional sincerity. It spoke of an intense yearning of the heart for the divine which is in Man and not in the temple, or scriptures, in images and symbols. The worshipper addresses his songs to Man the ideal, and says:

> Temples and mosques obstruct thy path,
> and I fail to hear thy call or to move,
> when the teachers and priest angrily crowd round
> me.

He does not follow any tradition of ceremony, but only believes in love. According to him

Love is the magic stone, that transmutes by its touch greed into sacrifice.

He goes on to say:

For the sake of this love heaven longs to become earth and gods to become man.

Since then I have often tried to meet these people, and sought to understand them through their songs, which are their only form of worship. One is often surprised to find in many of these verses a striking originality of sentiment and diction; for, at their best, they are spontaneously individual in their expressions. One such song is a hymn to the Ever Young. It exclaims:

O my flower buds, we worship the Young;
for the Young is the source of the holy Ganges of
     life;
from the Young flows the supreme bliss.

And it says:

We never offer ripe corn in the service of the Young,
nor fruit, nor seed,
but only the lotus bud which is of our own mind.
The young hour of the day, the morning,
is our time for the worship of Him
from whose contemplation has sprung the Universe.

It calls the Spirit of the Young the *Brahma Kamal*, "the infinite lotus". For it is something which has perfection in its heart and yet ever grows and unfolds its petals.

There have been men in India who never wrote learned texts about the religion of Man but had an overpowering desire and practical training for its attainment. They bore in their life the testimony of their intimacy with the Person who is in all persons, of Man the formless in the individual forms of men. Rajjab, a poet-saint of medieval India, says of Man:

> God-man (*nara-narayana*) is thy definition, it is not a delusion but truth. In thee the infinite seeks the finite, the perfect knowledge seeks love, and when the form and the Formless (the individual and the universal) are united love is fulfilled in devotion.

Ravidas, another poet of the same age, sings:

> Thou seest me, O Divine Man (*narahari*), and I see thee, and our love becomes mutual.

Of this God-man a village poet of Bengal says:

> He is within us, an unfathomable reality. We know him when we unlock our own self and meet in a true love with all others.

A brother poet of his says:

> Man seeks the man in me and I lose myself and run out.

And another singer sings of the Ideal Man, and says:

> How could the scripture know the meaning of the
> Lord who has his play in the world of human forms?
> Listen, O brother man (declares Chandidas), the
> truth of man is the highest truth, there is no other
> truth above it.

All these are proofs of a direct perception of humanity as an objective truth that rouses a profound feeling of longing and love. This is very unlike what we find in the intellectual cult of humanity, which is like a body that has tragically lost itself in the purgatory of shadows.

Wordsworth says:

> We live by admiration, hope and love,
> And ever as these are well and wisely fixed
> In dignity of being we ascend.

It is for dignity of being that we aspire through the expansion of our consciousness in a great reality of Man to which we belong. We realize it through admiration and love, through hope that soars beyond the actual, beyond our own span of life into an endless time wherein we live the life of all men.

This is the infinite perspective of human personality where man finds his religion. Science may include in its field of knowledge the starry world and the world beyond it; philosophy may try to find some universal principle which is at the root of all things, but religion inevitably concentrates itself on humanity, which illumines our reason, inspires our wisdom, stimulates our love, claims our intelligent service. There is an impersonal idea, which we call law, discoverable by an impersonal logic in its pursuit of the fathomless depth of the hydrogen atom and the distant virgin worlds clothed in eddying fire. But as the physiology of our beloved is not our beloved, so this impersonal law is not our God, the *Pitritamah pitrinam*, the Father who is ultimate in all fathers and mothers, of him we cannot say:

Tad viddhi pranipatena pariprasnena sevaya—

(Realize him by obeisance, by the desire to know, by service—)

For this can only be relevant to the God who is God and man at the same time; and if this faith be blamed for being anthropomorphic, then Man is to be blamed for being Man, and the lover for loving his dear one as a person instead of as a principle of psychology. We can never go beyond Man in all that we know and feel, and a mendicant singer of Bengal has said:

Our world is as it is in our comprehension; the thought and existence are commingled. Everything would be lost in unconsciousness if man were nought; and when response comes to your own call you know the meaning of reality.

According to him, what we call nature is not a philosophical abstraction, not cosmos, but what is revealed to *man* as nature. In fact it is included in himself and therefore there is a commingling of his mind with it, and in that he finds his own being. He is truly lessened in humanity if he cannot take it within him and through it feel the fulness of his own existence. His arts and literature are constantly giving expression to this intimate communion of man with his world. And the Vedic poet exclaims in his hymn to the sun:

Thou who nourishest the earth, who walkest alone,
O Sun, withdraw thy rays, reveal thy exceeding
beauty to me and let me realize that the Person who
is there is the One who I am.

It is for us to realize the Person who is in the heart of the All by the emancipated consciousness of our own personality. We know that the highest mission of science is to find the universe enveloped by the human comprehension; to see man's *visvarupa*, his great mental body, that touches the extreme verge of time and space, that includes the whole world within itself.

The original Aryans who came to India had for their gods the deities of rain, wind, fire, the cosmic forces which singularly enough found no definite shapes in images. A time came when it was recognized that individually they had no separate, unrelated power of their own, but there was one infinite source of power which was named Brahma. The cosmic divinity developed into an impersonal idea; what was physical grew into a metaphysical abstraction, even as in modern science matter vanishes into mathematics. And Brahma, according to those Indians, could neither be apprehended by mind nor described by words, even as matter in its ultimate analysis proves to be.

However satisfactory that idea might be as the unknowable principle relating to itself all the phenomena that are non-personal, it left the personal man in a void of negation. It cannot be gainsaid that we can never realize things in this world from inside, we can but know how they appear to us. In fact, in all knowledge we know our own self in its condition of knowledge. And religion sought the highest value of man's existence in this self. For this is the only truth of which he is immediately conscious from within. And he said:

Purushanna para kinchit
sa kashthta sa para gatih

(Nothing is greater than the Person;
he is the supreme, he is the ultimate goal.)

It is a village poet of East Bengal who preaches in a song the philosophical doctrine that the universe has its reality in its relation to the Person, which I translate in the following lines:

The sky and the earth are born of mine own eyes,
The hardness and softness, the cold and the heat are
    the products of mine own body,
The sweet smell and the bad are of my own nostrils.

This poet sings of the Eternal Person within him, coming out and appearing before his eyes, just as the Vedic Rishi speaks of the Person, who is in him, dwelling also in the heart of the sun:

I have seen the vision,
the vision of mine own revealing itself,
coming out from within me.

In India, there are those whose endeavour is to merge completely their personal self in an impersonal entity which is without any quality or definition; to reach a condition wherein mind becomes perfectly blank, losing all its activities. Those who claim the right to speak about it say that this is the purest state of consciousness, it is all joy and without any object or content. This is considered to be the ultimate end of *Yoga*, the cult of union, thus completely to identify one's being with the infinite Being who is beyond all thoughts and words. Such realization of transcendental consciousness accompanied by a perfect sense of bliss is a time-honoured tradition in our country, carrying in it the positive evidence which cannot be denied by any negative argument of refutation. Without disputing its truth I maintain that it may be valuable as a great psychological experience but all the same it is not religion, even as the knowledge of the ultimate state of the atom is of no use to an artist who deals in images in which atoms have taken forms. A certain condition of vacuum is needed for studying the state of things in its original purity, and the same may be said of the human spirit; but the original state is not necessarily the perfect state. The concrete form is a more perfect manifestation than the atom, and man is more perfect as a man than where he vanishes in an original indefiniteness. This is why the Ishopanishat says: "Truth is both finite and infinite at the same time, it moves and yet moves not, it is in the distant, also in the near, it is within all objects and without them."

This means that perfection as the ideal is immovable, but in its aspect of the real it constantly grows towards completion, it moves. And I say of the Supreme Man, that he is infinite in his essence, he is finite in his manifestation in us the individuals. As the Ishopanishat declares, a man must live his full term of life and work without greed, and thus realize himself in the Being who is in all beings. This means that he must reveal in his own personality the Supreme Person by his disinterested activities.

Chapter VIII

The Music Maker

A particle of sand would be nothing if it did not have its background in the whole physical world. This grain of sand is known in its context of the universe where we know all things through the testimony of our senses. When I say the grain of sand *is*, the whole physical world stands guarantee for the truth which is behind the appearance of the sand.

But where is that guarantee of truth for this personality of mine that has the mysterious faculty of knowledge before which the particle of sand offers its credential of identification? It must be acknowledged that this personal self of mine also has for its truth a background of personality where knowledge, unlike that of other things, can only be immediate and self-revealed.

What I mean by personality is a self-conscious principle of transcendental unity within man which comprehends all the details of facts that are individually his in knowledge and feeling, wish and will and work. In its negative aspect it is limited to the individual separateness, while in its positive aspect it ever extends itself in the infinite through the increase of its knowledge, love and activities.

And for this reason the most human of all facts about us is that we *do* dream of the limitless unattained—the dream which gives character to what *is* attained. Of all creatures man lives in an endless future. Our present is only a part of it. The ideas unborn, the unbodied spirits, tease our imagination with an insistence which makes them more real to our mind than things around us. The atmosphere of the future must always surround our present in order to make it life-bearing and suggestive of immortality. For he who has the healthy vigour of humanity in him has a strong instinctive faith that ideally he is limitless. That is why our greatest teachers claim from us a manifestation that touches the infinite. In this they pay homage to the Supreme Man. And our true worship lies in our indomitable courage to be great and thus to represent the human divine and ever to keep open the path of freedom towards the unattained.

We Indians have had the sad experience in our own part of the world how timid orthodoxy, its irrational repressions and its accumulation of dead centuries, dwarfs man through its idolatry of the past. Seated rigid in the centre of stagnation, it firmly ties the human spirit to the revolving wheels of habit till faintness overwhelms her. Like a sluggish stream choked by rotting weeds, it is divided into shallow slimy pools that shroud their dumbness in a narcotic mist of stupor. This mechanical spirit of tradition is essentially materialistic, it is blindly pious but not spiritual, obsessed by phantoms of unreason that haunt feeble minds in the ghastly disguise of religion. For our soul is shrunken when we allow foolish days to weave repeated patterns of unmeaning meshes round all departments of life. It becomes stunted when we have no object of profound interest, no prospect of heightened life, demanding clarity of mind and heroic attention to maintain and mature it. It is destroyed when we make fireworks of our animal passions for the enjoyment of their meteoric sensations, recklessly reducing to ashes all that could have been saved for permanent illumination. This happens not only to mediocre individuals hugging fetters that keep them irresponsible or hungering for lurid unrealities, but to generations of insipid races that have lost all emphasis of significance in themselves, having missed their future.

The continuous future is the domain of our millennium, which is with us more truly than what we see in our history in fragments of the present. It is in our dream. It is in the realm of the faith which creates perfection. We have seen the records of man's dream of the millennium, the ideal reality cherished by forgotten races in their admiration, hope and love manifested in the dignity of their being through some majesty in ideals and beauty in performance. While these races pass away one after another they leave great accomplishments behind them carrying their claim to recognition as dreamers—not so much as conquerors of earthly kingdoms, but as the designers of paradise. The poet gives us the best definition of man when he says:

> We are the music-makers,
> We are the dreamers of dreams.

Our religions present for us the dreams of the ideal unity which is man himself as he manifests the infinite. We suffer from the sense of sin, which is the sense of discord, when any disruptive passion tears gaps in our vision of the One in man, creating isolation in our self from the universal humanity.

The Upanishad says, *Ma gridah*, "Covet not". For coveting

diverts attention from the infinite value of our personality to the temptation of materials. Our village poet sings: "Man will brightly flash into your sight, my heart, if you shut the door of desires."

We have seen how primitive man was occupied with his physical needs, and thus restricted himself to the present which is the time boundary of the animal; and he missed the urge of his consciousness to seek its emancipation in a world of ultimate human value.

Modern civilization for the same reason seems to turn itself back to that primitive mentality. Our needs have multiplied so furiously fast that we have lost our leisure for the deeper realization of our self and our faith in it. It means that we have lost our religion, the longing for the touch of the divine in man, the builder of the heaven, the music-maker, the dreamer of dreams. This has made it easy to tear into shreds our faith in the perfection of the human ideal, in its wholeness, as the fuller meaning of reality. No doubt it is wonderful that music contains a fact which has been analysed and measured, and which music shares in common with the braying of an ass or of a motor-car horn. But it is still more wonderful that music has a truth, which cannot be analysed into fractions; and there the difference between it and the bellowing impertinence of a motor-car horn is infinite. Men of our own times have analysed the human mind, its dreams, its spiritual aspirations,—most often caught unawares in the shattered state of madness, disease and desultory dreams—and they have found to their satisfaction that these are composed of elemental animalities tangled into various knots. This may be an important discovery; but what is still more important to realize is the fact that by some miracle of creation man infinitely transcends the component parts of his own character.

Suppose that some psychological explorer suspects that man's devotion to his beloved has at bottom our primitive stomach's hankering for human flesh; we need not contradict him; for whatever may be its genealogy, its secret composition, the complete character of our love, in its perfect mingling of physical, mental and spiritual associations, is unique in its utter difference from cannibalism. The truth underlying the possibility of such transmutation is the truth of our religion. A lotus has in common with a piece of rotten flesh the elements of carbon and hydrogen. In a state of dissolution there is no difference between them, but in a state of creation the difference is immense; and it is that difference which really matters. We are told that some of our most sacred sentiments hold hidden in them instincts contrary to what these sentiments profess to be. Such disclosures have the effect upon certain persons of the relief of a tension, even like the relaxation in death of the incessant strenuousness of life.

We find in modern literature that something like a chuckle of an exultant disillusionment is becoming contagious, and the knights-errant of the cult of arson are abroad, setting fire to our time-honoured altars of worship, proclaiming that the images enshrined on them, even if beautiful, are made of mud. They say that it has been found out that the appearances in human idealism are deceptive, that the underlying mud is real. From such a point of view, the whole of creation may be said to be a gigantic deception, and the billions of revolving electric specks that have the appearance of "you" or "me" should be condemned as bearers of false evidence.

But whom do they seek to delude? If it be beings like ourselves who possess some inborn criterion of the real, then to them these very appearances in their integrity must represent reality, and not their component electric specks. For them the rose must be more satisfactory as an object than its constituent gases, which can be tortured to speak against the evident identity of the rose. The rose, even like the human sentiment of goodness, or ideal of beauty, belongs to the realm of creation, in which all its rebellious elements are reconciled in a perfect harmony. Because these elements in their simplicity yield themselves to our scrutiny, we in our pride are inclined to give them the best prizes as actors in that mystery-play, the rose. Such an analysis is really only giving a prize to our own detective cleverness.

I repeat again that the sentiments and ideals which man in his process of self-creation has built up, should be recognized in their wholeness. In all our faculties or passions there is nothing which is absolutely good or bad; they all are the constituents of the great human personality. They are notes that are wrong when in wrong places; our education is to make them into chords that may harmonize with the grand music of Man. The animal in the savage has been transformed into higher stages in the civilized man—in other words has attained a truer consonance with Man the divine, not through any elimination of the original materials, but through a magical grouping of them, through the severe discipline of art, the discipline of curbing and stressing in proper places, establishing a balance of lights and shadows in the background and foreground, and thus imparting a unique value to our personality in all its completeness.

So long as we have faith in this value, our energy is steadily sustained in its creative activity that reveals the eternal Man.

This faith is helped on all sides by literature, arts, legends, symbols, ceremonials, by the remembrance of heroic souls who have personified it in themselves.

Our religion is the inner principle that comprehends these endeavours and expressions and dreams through which we approach Him in whose image we are made. To keep alive our faith in the reality of the ideal perfection is the function of civilization, which is mainly formed of sentiments and the images that represent that ideal. In other words, civilization is a creation of art, created for the objective realization of our vision of the spiritually perfect. It is the product of the art of religion. We stop its course of conquest when we accept the cult of realism and forget that realism is the worst form of untruth, because it contains a minimum of truth. It is like preaching that only in the morgue can we comprehend the reality of the human body— the body which has its perfect revelation when seen in life. All great human facts are surrounded by an immense atmosphere of expectation. They are never complete if we leave out from them what might be, what should be, what is not yet proven but profoundly felt, what points towards the immortal. This dwells in a perpetual surplus in the individual, that transcends all the desultory facts about him.

The realism in Man is the animal in him, whose life is a mere duration of time; the human in him is his reality which has life everlasting for its background. Rocks and crystals being complete definitely in what they are, can keep as "mute insensate things" a kind of dumb dignity in their stolidly limited realism; while human facts grow unseemly and diseased, breeding germs of death, when divested of their creative ideal—the ideal of Man the divine. The difference between the notes as mere facts of sound and music, as a truth of expression is immense.

For music, though it comprehends a limited number of notes, yet represents the infinite. It is for man to produce the music of the spirit with all the notes which he has in his psychology and which, through inattention or perversity, can easily be translated into a frightful noise. In music man is revealed, and not in a noise.

Chapter IX

The Artist

THE fundamental desire of life is the desire to exist. It claims from us a vast amount of training and experience about the necessaries of livelihood. Yet it does not cost me much to confess that the food that I have taken, the dress that I wear, the house where I have my lodging, represent a stupendous knowledge, practice and organization which I helplessly lack; for I find that I am not altogether despised for such ignorance and inefficiency. Those who read me seem fairly satisfied that I am nothing better than a poet or perhaps a philosopher—which latter reputation I do not claim and dare not hold through the precarious help of misinformation.

It is quite evident in spite of my deficiency that in human society I represent a vocation, which though superfluous has yet been held worthy of commendation. In fact, I am encouraged in my rhythmic futility by being offered moral and material incentives for its cultivation. If a foolish blackbird did not know how to seek its food, to build its nest, or to avoid its enemies, but specialized in singing, its fellow creatures, urged by their own science of genetics, would dutifully allow it to starve and perish. That I am not treated in a similar fashion is the evidence of an immense difference between the animal existence and the civilization of man. His great distinction dwells in the indefinite margin of life in him which affords a boundless background for his dreams and creations. And it is in this realm of freedom that he realizes his divine dignity, his great human truth, and is pleased when I as a poet sing victory to him, to Man the self-revealer, who goes on exploring ages of creation to find himself in perfection.

Reality, in all its manifestations, reveals itself in the emotional and imaginative background of our mind. We know it, not because we can think of it, but because we directly feel it. And therefore, even if rejected by the logical mind, it is not banished from our consciousness. As an incident it may be beneficial or injurious, but as a revelation its value lies in the fact that it offers us an experience through emotion or imagination; we feel ourselves in a special field of realization. This feeling itself is delightful when it is not accompanied by any great physical or moral risk; we love to feel even fear or sorrow if it is detached from all practical consequences. This is the reason of our enjoyment of tragic dramas, in which the feeling of pain rouses our consciousness to a white heat of intensity.

The reality of my own self is immediate and indubitable to me. Whatever else affects me in a like manner is real for myself, and it inevitably attracts and occupies my attention for its own sake, blends itself with my personality, making it richer and larger and causing it delight. My friend may not be beautiful, useful, rich or great, but he is real to me; in him I feel my own extension and my joy.

The consciousness of the real within me seeks for its own

corroboration the touch of the Real outside me. When it fails the self in me is depressed. When our surroundings are monotonous and insignificant, having no emotional reaction upon our mind, we become vague to ourselves. For we are like pictures, whose reality is helped by the background if it is sympathetic. The punishment we suffer in solitary confinement consists in the obstruction to the relationship between the world of reality and the real in ourselves, causing the latter to become indistinct in a haze of inactive imagination: our personality is blurred, we miss the companionship of our own being through the diminution of our self. The world of our knowledge is enlarged for us through the extension of our information; the world of our personality grows in its area with a large and deeper experience of our personal self in our own universe through sympathy and imagination.

As this world, that can be known through knowledge, is limited to us owing to our ignorance, so the world of personality, that can be realized by our own personal self, is also restricted by the limit of our sympathy and imagination. In the dim twilight of insensitiveness a large part of our world remains to us like a procession of nomadic shadows. According to the stages of our consciousness we have more or less been able to identify ourselves with this world, if not as a whole, at least in fragments; and our enjoyment dwells in that wherein we feel ourselves thus united. In art we express the delight of this unity by which this world is realized as humanly significant to us. I have my physical, chemical and biological self; my knowledge of it extends through the extension of my knowledge of the physical, chemical and biological world. I have my personal self, which has its communication with our feelings, sentiments and imaginations, which lends itself to be coloured by our desires and shaped by our imageries.

Science urges us to occupy by our mind the immensity of the knowable world; our spiritual teacher, enjoins us to comprehend by our soul the infinite Spirit which is in the depth of the moving and changing facts of the world; the urging of our artistic nature is to realize the manifestation of personality in the world of appearance, the reality of existence which is in harmony with the real within us. Where this harmony is not deeply felt, there we are aliens and perpetually homesick. For man by nature is an artist; he never receives passively and accurately in his mind a physical representation of things around him. There goes on a continual adaptation, a transformation of facts into human imagery, through constant touches of his sentiments and imagination. The animal has the geography of its birthplace; man has his country, the geography of his personal self. The vision of it is not merely physical; it has its artistic unity, it is a perpetual creation. In his country, his consciousness being unobstructed, man extends his relationship, which is of his own creative personality. In order to live efficiently man must know facts and their laws. In order to be happy he must establish harmonious relationship with all things with which he has dealings. Our creation is the modification of relationship.

The great men who appear in our history remain in our mind not as a static fact but as a living historical image. The sublime suggestions of their lives become blended into a noble consistency in legends made living in the life of ages. Those men with whom we live we constantly modify in our minds, making them more real to us than they would be in a bare presentation. Men's ideal of womanhood and women's ideal of manliness are created by the imagination through a mental grouping of qualities and conducts according to our hopes and desires, and men and women consciously and unconsciously strive towards its attainment. In fact, they reach a degree of reality for each other according to their success in adapting these respective ideals to their own nature. To say that these ideals are imaginary and therefore not true is wrong in man's case. His true life is in his own creation, which represents the infinity of man. He is naturally indifferent to things that merely exist; they must have some ideal value for him, and then only his consciousness fully recognizes them as real. Men are never true in their isolated self, and their imagination is the faculty that brings before their mind the vision of their own greater being.

We can make truth ours by actively modulating its interrelations. This is the work of art; for reality is not based in the substance of things but in the principal of relationship. Truth is the infinite pursued by metaphysics; fact is the infinite pursued by science, while reality is the definition of the infinite which relates truth to the person. Reality is human; it is what we are conscious of, by which we are affected, that which we express. When we are intensely aware of it, we are aware of ourselves and it gives us delight. We live in it, we always widen its limits. Our arts and literature represent this creative activity which is fundamental in man.

But the mysterious fact about it is that though the individuals are separately seeking their expression, their success is never individualistic in character. Men must find and feel and represent in all their creative works Man the Eternal, the creator. Their civilization is a continual discovery of the transcendental humanity. In whatever it fails it shows the failure of the artist, which is the failure in expression; and that civilization perishes in which the individual thwarts the revelation of the universal. For Reality is the truth of Man, who belongs to all times, and any individualistic madness of men against Man cannot thrive for long.

Man is eager that his feeling for what is real to him must never die; it must find an imperishable form. The consciousness of this self of mine is so intensely evident to me that it assumes the character of immortality. I cannot imagine that it ever has been or can be non-existent. In a similar manner all things that are real to me are for myself eternal, and therefore worthy of a language that has a permanent meaning. We know individuals who have the habit of inscribing their names on the walls of some majestic monument of architecture. It is a pathetic way of associating their own names with some works of art which belong to all times and to all men. Our hunger for reputation comes from our desire to make objectively real that which is inwardly real to us. He who is inarticulate is insignificant, like a dark star that cannot prove itself. He ever waits for the artist to give him his fullest worth, not for anything specially excellent in him but for the wonderful fact that he is what he certainly is, that he carries in him the eternal mystery of being.

A Chinese friend of mine while travelling with me in the streets of Peking suddenly exclaimed with a vehement enthusiasm: "Look, here is a donkey!" Surely it was an utterly ordinary donkey, like an indisputable truism, needing no special introduction from him. I was amused; but it made me think. This animal is generally classified as having certain qualities that are not recommendable and then hurriedly dismissed. It was obscured to me by an envelopment of commonplace associations; I was lazily certain that I knew it and therefore I hardly saw it. But my friend, who possessed the artist mind of China, did not treat it with a cheap knowledge but could see it afresh and recognize it as real. When I say real, I mean that it did not remain at the outskirt of his consciousness tied to a narrow definition, but it easily blended in his imagination, produced a vision, a special harmony of lines, colours and life and movement, and became intimately his own. The admission of a donkey into a drawing-room is violently opposed; yet there is no prohibition against its finding a place in a picture which may be admiringly displayed on the drawing-room wall.

The only evidence of truth in art exists when it compels us to say, "I see." A donkey we may pass by in Nature, but a donkey in art we must acknowledge even if it be a creature that disreputably ignores all its natural history responsibility, even if it resembles a mushroom in its head and a palm-leaf in its tail.

In the Upanishad it is said in a parable that there are two birds sitting on the same bough, one of which feeds and the other looks on. This is an image of the mutual relationship of the infinite being and the finite self. The delight of the bird which looks on is great, for it is a pure and free delight. There are both of these birds in man himself, the objective one with its business of life, the subjective one with its disinterested joy of vision.

A child comes to me and commands me to tell her a story. I tell her of a tiger which is disgusted with the black stripes on its body and comes to my frightened servant demanding a piece of soap. The story gives my little audience immense pleasure, the pleasure of a vision, and her mind cries out, "It is here, for I see!" She knows a tiger in the book of natural history, but she can see the tiger in the story of mine.

I am sure that even this child of five knows that it is an impossible tiger that is out on its untigerly quest of an absurd soap. The delightfulness of the tiger for her is not in its beauty, its usefulness, or its probability; but in the undoubted fact that she can see it in her mind with a greater clearness of vision than she can the walls around her—the walls that brutally shout their evidence of certainty which is merely circumstantial. The tiger in the story is inevitable, it has the character of a complete image, which offers its testimonial of truth in itself. The listener's own mind is the eyewitness, whose direct experience could not be contradicted. A tiger must be like every other tiger in order that it may have its place in a book of Science; there it must be a commonplace tiger to be at all tolerated. But in the story it is uncommon, it can never be reduplicated. We *know* a thing because it belongs to a class; we *see* a thing because it belongs to itself. The tiger of the story completely detached itself from all others of its kind and easily assumed a distinct individuality in the heart of the listener. The child could vividly see it, because by the help of her imagination it became her own tiger, one with herself, and this union of the subject and object gives us joy. Is it because there is no separation between them in truth, the separation being the *Maya*, which is creation?

There come in our history occasions when the consciousness of a large multitude becomes suddenly illumined with the recognition of a reality which rises far above the dull obviousness of daily happenings. The world becomes vivid; we see, we feel it with all our soul. Such an occasion there was when the voice of Buddha reached distant shores across physical and moral impediments. Then our life and our world found their profound meaning of reality in their relation to the central person who offered us emancipation of love. Men, in order to make this great human experience ever memorable, determined to do the impossible; they made rocks to speak, stones to sing, caves to remember; their cry of joy and hope took immortal forms along the hills and deserts, across barren solitudes and populous cities. A gigantic creative endeavour built up its triumph in stupendous carvings, defying obstacles that were over-whelming. Such heroic activity over the greater part of the Eastern continents clearly answers the question: "What is Art?" It is the response of man's creative soul to the call of the Real.

Once there came a time, centuries ago in Bengal, when the divine love drama that has made its eternal playground in human souls was vividly revealed by a personality radiating its intimate realization of God. The mind of a whole people was stirred by a vision of the world as an instrument, through which sounded out invitation to the meeting of bliss. The ineffable mystery of God's love-call, taking shape in an endless panorama of colours and forms, inspired activity in music that overflowed the restrictions of classical conventionalism. Our Kirtan music of Bengal came to its being like a star flung up by a burning whirlpool of emotion in the heart of a whole people, and their consciousness was aflame with a sense of reality that must be adequately acknowledged.

The question may be asked as to what place music occupies in my theory that art is for evoking in our mind the deep sense of reality in its richest aspect. Music is the most abstract of all the arts, as mathematics is in the region of science. In fact these two have a deep relationship with each other. Mathematics is the logic of numbers and dimensions. It is therefore employed as the basis of our scientific knowledge. When taken out of its concrete associations and reduced to symbols, it reveals its grand structural majesty, the inevitableness of its own perfect concord. Yet there is not merely a logic but also a magic of mathematics which works at the world of appearance, producing harmony—the cadence of inter-relationship. This rhythm of harmony has been extracted from its usual concrete context, and exhibited through the medium of sound. And thus the pure essence of expressiveness in existence is offered in music. Expressiveness finds the least resistance in sound, having freedom unencumbered by the burden of facts and thoughts. This gives it a power to arouse in us an intimate feeling of reality. In the pictorial, plastic and literary arts, the object and our feelings with regard to it are closely associated, like the rose and its perfumes. In music, the feeling distilled in sound becomes itself an independent object. It assumes a tune-form which is definite, but a meaning which is undefinable, and yet which grips our mind with a sense of absolute truth.

It is the magic of mathematics, the rhythm which is in the heart of all creation, which moves in the atom and, in its different measures, fashions gold and lead, the rose and the thorn, the sun and the planets. These are the dance-steps of numbers in the arena of time and space, which weave the *maya*, the patterns of appearance, the incessant flow of change, that ever is and is not. It is the rhythm that churns up images from the vague and makes tangible what is elusive. This is *maya*, this is the art in creation, and art in literature, which is the magic of rhythm.

And must we stop here? What we know as intellectual truth, is that also not a rhythm of the relationship of facts, that weaves the pattern of theory, and produces a sense of convincingness to a person who somehow feels sure that he knows the truth? We believe any fact to be true because of a harmony, a rhythm in reason, the process of which is analysable by the logic of mathematics, but not its result in me, just as we can count the notes but cannot account for the music. The mystery is that I am convinced, and this also belongs to the *maya* of creation, whose one important, indispensable factor is this self-conscious personality that I represent.

And the Other? I believe it is also a self-conscious personality, which has its eternal harmony with mine.

Chapter X

Man's Nature

FROM the time when Man became truly conscious of his own self he also became conscious of a mysterious spirit of unity which found its manifestation through him in his society. It is a subtle medium of relationship between individuals, which is not for any utilitarian purpose but for its own ultimate truth, not a sum of arithmetic but a value of life. Somehow Man has felt that this comprehensive spirit of unity has a divine character which could claim the sacrifice of all that is individual in him, that in it dwells his highest meaning transcending his limited self, representing his best freedom.

Man's reverential loyalty to this spirit of unity is expressed in his religion; it is symbolized in the names of his deities. That is why, in the beginning, his gods were tribal gods, even gods of the different communities belonging to the same tribe. With the extension of the consciousness of human unity his God became revealed to him as one and universal, proving that the truth of human unity is the truth of Man's God.

In the Sanskrit language, religion goes by the name *dharma*, which in the derivative meaning implies the principle of relationship that holds us firm, and in its technical sense means the virtue of a thing, the essential quality of it; for instance, heat is the essential quality of fire, though in certain of its stages it may be absent.

Religion consists in the endeavour of men to cultivate and express those qualities which are inherent in the nature of Man the Eternal, and to have faith in him. If these qualities were absolutely natural in individuals, religion could have no purpose. We begin our history with all the original promptings of our brute nature which helps us to fulfil those vital needs of ours that are immediate. But deeper within us there is a current of tendencies which runs in many ways in a contrary direction, the life current of universal humanity. Religion has its function in reconciling the contradiction, by subordinating the brute nature to what we consider as the truth of Man. This is helped when our faith in the Eternal Man, whom we call by different names and imagine in different images, is made strong. The contradiction between the two natures in us is so great that men have willingly sacrificed their vital needs and courted death in order to express their *dharma*, which represents the truth of the Supreme Man.

The vision of the Supreme Man is realized by our imagination, but not created by our mind. More real than individual men, he surpasses each of us in his permeating personality which is transcendental. The procession of his ideas, following his great purpose, is ever moving across obstructive facts towards the perfected truth. We, the individuals, having our place in his composition, may or may not be in conscious harmony with his purpose, may even put obstacles in his path bringing down our doom upon ourselves. But we gain our true religion when we consciously co-operate with him, finding our exceeding joy through suffering and sacrifice. For through our own love for him we are made conscious of a great love that radiates from his being, who is Mahatma, the Supreme Spirit.

The great Chinese sage Lao-Tze has said: "One who may die, but will not perish, has life everlasting". It means that he lives in the life of the immortal Man. The urging for this life induces men to go through the struggle for a true survival. And it has been said in our scripture: "Through *adharma* (the negation of *dharma*) man prospers, gains what appears desirable, conquers enemies, but he perishes at the root." In this saying it is suggested that there is a life which is truer for men than their physical life which is transient.

Our life gains what is called "value" in those of its aspects which represent eternal humanity in knowledge, in sympathy, in deeds, in character and creative works. And from the beginning of our history we are seeking, often at the cost of everything else, the value for our life and not merely success; in other words, we are trying to realize in ourselves the immortal Man, so that we may die but not perish. This is the meaning of the utterance in the Upanishad: "*Tam vedyam purusham veda, yatha ma vo mrityuh parivyathah*"—"Realize the Person so that thou mayst not suffer from death."

The meaning of these words is highly paradoxical, and cannot be proved by our senses or our reason, and yet its influence is so strong in men that they have cast away all fear and greed, defied all the instincts that cling to the brute nature, for the sake of acknowledging and preserving a life which belongs to the

Eternal Person. It is all the more significant because many of them do not believe in its reality, and yet are ready to fling away for it all that they believe to be final and the only positive fact.

We call this ideal reality "spiritual". That word is vague; nevertheless, through the dim light which reaches us across the barriers of physical existence, we seem to have a stronger faith in the spiritual Man than in the physical; and from the dimmest period of his history, Man has a feeling that the apparent facts of existence are not final; that his supreme welfare depends upon his being able to remain in perfect relationship with some great mystery behind the veil, at the threshold of a larger life, which is for giving him a far higher value than a mere continuation of his physical life in the material world.

Our physical body has its comprehensive reality in the physical world, which may be truly called our universal body, without which our individual body would miss its function. Our physical life realizes its growing meaning through a widening freedom in its relationship with the physical world, and this gives it a greater happiness than the mere pleasure of satisfied needs. We become aware of a profound meaning of our own self at the consciousness of some ideal of perfection, some truth beautiful or majestic which gives us an inner sense of completeness, a heightened sense of our own reality. This strengthens man's faith, effective even if indefinite—his faith in an objective ideal of perfection comprehending the human world. His vision of it has been beautiful or distorted, luminous or obscure, according to the stages of development that his consciousness has attained. But whatever may be the name and nature of his religious creed, man's ideal of human perfection has been based upon a bond of unity running through individuals culminating in a supreme Being who represents the eternal In human personality. In his civilization the perfect expression of this idea produces the wealth of truth which is for the revelation of Man and not merely for the success of life. But when this creative ideal which is *dharma* gives place to some overmastering passion in a large body of men civilization bursts out in an explosive flame, like a star that has lighted its own funeral pyre of boisterous brilliancy.

When I was a child I had the freedom to make my own toys out of trifles and create my own games from imagination. In my happiness my playmates had their full share, in fact the complete enjoyment of my games depended upon their taking part in them. One day, in this paradise of our childhood, entered the temptation from the market world of the adult. A toy brought from an English shop was given to one of our companions; it was perfect, it was big and wonderfully lifelike. He became proud of the toy and less mindful of the game; he kept that expensive thing carefully away from us, glorying in his exclusive possession of it, feeling himself superior to his playmates whose toys were cheap. I am sure if he could use the modern language of history he would say that he was more civilized than ourselves to the extent of his owning that ridiculously perfect toy.

One thing he failed to realize in his excitement—a fact which at the moment seemed to him insignificant—that this temptation obscured something a great deal more perfect than his toy, the revelation of the perfect child which ever dwells in the heart of man, in other words, the *dharma* of the child. The toy merely expressed his wealth but not himself, not the child's creative spirit, not the child's generous joy in his play, his identification of himself with others who were his compeers in his play world. Civilization is to express Man's *dharma* and not merely his cleverness, power and possession.

Once there was an occasion for me to motor down to Calcutta from a place a hundred miles away. Something wrong with the mechanism made it necessary for us to have a repeated supply of water almost every half-hour. At the first village where we were compelled to stop, we asked the help of a man to find water for us. It proved quite a task for him, but when we offered him his reward, poor though he was, he refused to accept it. In fifteen other villages the same thing happened. In a hot country, where travellers constantly need water and where the water supply grows scanty in summer, the villagers consider it their duty to offer water to those who need it. They could easily make a business out of it, following the inexorable law of demand and supply. But the ideal which they consider to be their *dharma* has become one with their life. They do not claim any personal merit for possessing it.

Lao-Tze, speaking about the man who is truly good, says: "He quickens but owns not. He acts but claims not. Merit he accomplishes but dwells not in it. Since he does not dwell in it, it will never leave him." That which is outside ourselves we can sell; but that which is one with our being we cannot sell. This complete assimilation of truth belongs to the paradise of perfection; it lies beyond the purgatory of self-consciousness. To have reached it proves a long process of civilization.

To be able to take a considerable amount of trouble in order to supply water to a passing stranger and yet never to claim merit or reward for it seems absurdly and negligibly simple compared with the capacity to produce an amazing number of things per minute. A millionaire tourist, ready to corner the food market and grow rich by driving the whole world to the brink of starvation, is sure to feel too superior to notice this simple thing while rushing through our villages at sixty miles an hour.

Yes, it is simple, as simple as it is for a gentleman to be a gentleman; but that simplicity is the product of centuries of culture. That simplicity is difficult of imitation. In a few years' time, it might be possible for me to learn how to make holes in thousands of needles simultaneously by turning a wheel, but to be absolutely simple in one's hospitality to one's enemy, or to a stranger, requires generations of training. Simplicity takes no account of its own value, claims no wages, and therefore those who are enamoured of power do not realize that simplicity of spiritual expression is the highest product of civilization.

A process of disintegration can kill this rare fruit of a higher life, as a whole race of birds possessing some rare beauty can be made extinct by the vulgar power of avarice which has civilized weapons. This fact was clearly proved to me when I found that the only place where a price was expected for the water given to us was a suburb at Calcutta, where life was richer, the water supply easier and more abundant and where progress flowed in numerous channels in all directions. It shows that a harmony of character which the people once had was lost—the harmony with the inner self which is greater in its universality than the self that gives prominence to its personal needs. The latter loses its feeling of beauty and generosity in its calculation of profit; for there it represents exclusively itself and not the universal Man.

There is an utterance in the Atharva Veda, wherein appears the question as to who it was that gave Man his music. Birds repeat their single notes, or a very simple combination of them, but Man builds his world of music and establishes ever new rhythmic relationship of notes. These reveal to him a universal mystery of creation which cannot be described. They bring to him the inner rhythm that transmutes facts into truths. They give him pleasure not merely for his sense of hearing, but for his deeper being, which gains satisfaction in the ideal of perfect unity. Somehow man feels that truth finds its body in such perfection; and when he seeks for his own best revelation he seeks a medium which has the harmonious unity, as has music. Our impulse to give expression to Universal Man produces arts and literature. They in their cadence of lines, colours, movements, words, thoughts, express vastly more than what they appear to be on the surface. They open the windows of our mind to the eternal reality of man. They are the superfluity of wealth of which we claim our common inheritance whatever may be the country and time to which we belong; for they are inspired by the universal mind. And not merely in his arts, but in his own behaviour, the individual must for his excellence give emphasis to an ideal which has some value of truth that ideally belongs to all men. In other words, he should create a music of expression in his conduct and surroundings which makes him represent the supreme Personality. And civilization is the creation of the race, its expression of the universal Man.

When I first visited Japan I had the opportunity of observing where the two parts of the human sphere strongly contrasted; one, on which grew up the ancient continents of social ideal, standards of beauty, codes of personal behaviour; and the other part, the fluid element, the perpetual current that carried wealth to its shores from all parts of the world. In half a century's time Japan has been able to make her own the mighty spirit of progress which suddenly burst upon her one morning in a storm of insult and menace. China also has had her rousing, when her self-respect was being knocked to pieces through series of helpless years, and I am sure she also will master before long the instrument which hurt her to the quick. But the ideals that imparted life and body to Japanese civilization had been nourished in the reverent hopes of countless generations through ages which were not primarily occupied in an incessant hunt for opportunities. They had those large tracts of leisure in them which are necessary for the blossoming of Life's beauty and the ripening of her wisdom.

On the one hand we can look upon the modern factories in Japan with their numerous mechanical organizations and engines of production and destruction of the latest type. On the other hand, against them we may see some fragile vase, some small piece of silk, some architecture of sublime simplicity, some perfect lyric of bodily movement. We may also notice the Japanese expression of courtesy daily extracting from them a considerable amount of time and trouble. All these have come not from any accurate knowledge of things but from an intense consciousness of the value of reality which takes time for its fullness. What Japan reveals in her skilful manipulation of telegraphic wires and railway lines, of machines for manufacturing things and for killing men, is more or less similar to what we see in other countries which have similar opportunity for training. But in her art of living, her pictures, her code of conduct, the various forms of beauty which her religious and social ideals assume, Japan expresses her own personality, her *dharma*, which, in order to be of any worth, must be unique and at the same time represent Man of the Everlasting Life.

Lao-Tze has said: "Not knowing the eternal causes passions to rise; and that is evil." He has also said: "Let us die, and yet not perish." For we die when we lose our physical life, we perish when we miss our humanity. And humanity is the *dharma* of human beings.

What is evident in this world is the endless procession of

moving things; but what is to be realized is the supreme human Truth by which the human world is permeated.

We must never forget to-day that a mere movement is not valuable in itself, that it may be a sign of a dangerous form of inertia. We must be reminded that a great upheaval of spirit, a universal realization of true dignity of man once caused by Buddha's teachings in India, started a movement for centuries which produced illumination of literature, art, science and numerous efforts of public beneficence. This was a movement whose motive force was not some additional accession of knowledge or power or urging of some overwhelming passion. It was an inspiration for freedom, the freedom which enables us to realize *dharma*, the truth of Eternal Man.

Lao-Tze in one of his utterances has said: "Those who have virtue (*dharma*) attend to their obligations; those who have no virtue attend to their claims." Progress which is not related to an inner *dharma*, but no an attraction which is external, seeks to satisfy our endless claims. But civilization, which is an ideal, gives us the abundant power to renounce which is the power that realizes the infinite and inspires creation.

This great Chinese sage has said: "To increase life is called a blessing." For the increase of life realizes the eternal life and yet does not transcend the limits of life's unity. The mountain pine grows tall and great, its every inch maintains the rhythm of an inner balance, and therefore even in its seeming extravagance it has the reticent grace of self-control. The tree and its productions belong to the same vital system of cadence; the timber, the flowers, leaves and fruits are one with the tree; their exuberance is not a malady of exaggeration, but a blessing.

Chapter XI

The Meeting

OUR great prophets in all ages did truly realize in themselves the freedom of the soul in their consciousness of the spiritual kinship of man which is universal. And yet human races, owing to their external geographical condition, developed in their individual isolation a mentality that is obnoxiously selfish. In their instinctive search for truth in religion either they dwarfed and deformed it in the mould of the primitive distortions of their own race-mind, or else they shut their God within temple walls and scriptural texts safely away, especially from those departments of life where his absence gives easy access to devil-worship in various names and forms. They treated their God in the same way as in some forms of government the King is treated, who has traditional honour but no effective authority. The true meaning of God has remained vague in our minds only because our consciousness of the spiritual unity has been thwarted.

One of the potent reasons for this—our geographical separation—has now been nearly removed. Therefore the time has come when we must, for the sake of truth and for the sake of that peace which is the harvest of truth, refuse to allow the idea of our God to remain indistinct behind unrealities of formal rites and theological mistiness.

The creature that lives its life screened and sheltered in a dark cave, finds its safety in the very narrowness of its own environment. The economical providence of Nature curtails and tones down its sensibilities to such a limited necessity. But if these cave-walls were to become suddenly removed by some catastrophe, then either it must accept the doom of extinction, or carry on satisfactory negotiations with its wider surroundings.

The races of mankind will never again be able to go back to their citadels of high-walled exclusiveness. They are today exposed to one another, physically and intellectually. The shells which have so long given them full security within their individual enclosures have been broken, and by no artificial process can they be mended again. So we have to accept this fact, even though we have not yet fully adapted our minds to this changed environment of publicity, even though through it we may have to run all the risks entailed by the wider expansion of life's freedom.

A large part of our tradition is our code of adjustment which deals with the circumstances special to ourselves. These traditions, no doubt, variegate the several racial personalities with their distinctive colours—colours which have their poetry and also certain protective qualities suitable to each different environment. We may come to acquire a strong love for our own colourful race speciality; but if that gives us fitness only for a very narrow world, then at the slightest variation in our outward circumstances we may have to pay for this love with our life itself.

In the animal world there are numerous instances of complete race-suicide overtaking those who fondly clung to some advantage which later on became a hindrance in an altered dispensation. In fact the superiority of man is proved by his adaptability to extreme surprises of chance—neither the torrid nor the frigid zone of his destiny offering him insuperable obstacles.

The vastness of the race problem with which we are faced to-day will either compel us to train ourselves to moral fitness in the place of merely external efficiency, or the complications arising out of it will fetter all our movements and drag us to our death.

When our necessity becomes urgently insistent, when the resources that have sustained us so long are exhausted, then our spirit puts forth all its force to discover some other source of sustenance deeper and more permanent. This leads us from the exterior to the interior of our storehouse. When muscle does not fully serve us, we come to awaken intellect to ask for its help and are then surprised to find in it a greater source of strength for us than physical power. When, in their turn, our intellectual gifts grow perverse, and only help to render our suicide gorgeous and exhaustive, our soul must seek an alliance with some power which is still deeper, yet further removed from the rude stupidity of muscle.

Hitherto the cultivation of intense race egotism is the one thing that has found its fullest scope at this meeting of men. In no period of human history has there been such an epidemic of moral perversity, such a universal churning up of jealousy, greed, hatred and mutual suspicion. Every people, weak or strong, is constantly indulging in a violent dream of rendering itself thoroughly hurtful to others. In this galloping competition of hurtfulness, on the slope of a bottomless pit, no nation dares to stop or slow down. A scarlet fever with a raging temperature has attacked the entire body of mankind, and political passion has taken the place of creative personality in all departments of life.

It is well known that when greed has for its object material gain then it can have no end. It is like the chasing of the horizon by a lunatic. To go on in a competition multiplying millions becomes a steeplechase of insensate futility that has obstacles but no goal. It has for its parallel the fight with material weapons—weapons which must perpetually be multiplied, opening up new vistas of destruction and evoking new forms of insanity in the forging of frightfulness. Thus seems now to have commenced the last fatal adventure of drunken Passion riding on an intellect of prodigious power.

To-day, more than ever before in our history, the aid of spiritual power is needed. Therefore I believe its resources will surely be discovered in the hidden depths of our being. Pioneers will come to take up this adventure and suffer, and through suffering open out a path to that higher elevation of life in which lies our safety.

Let me, in reference to this, give an instance from the history of Ancient India. There was a noble period in the early days of India when, to a band of dreamers, agriculture appeared as a great idea and not merely useful fact. The heroic personality of Ramachandra, who espoused its cause, was sung in popular ballads, which in a later age forgot their original message and were crystallized into an epic merely extolling some domestic virtues of its hero. It is quite evident, however, from the legendary relics lying entombed in the story, that a new age ushered in by the spread of agriculture came as a divine voice to those who could hear. It lifted up the primeval screen of the wilderness, brought the distant near, and broke down all barricades.

Men who had formed separate and antagonistic groups in their sheltered seclusions were called upon to form a united people.

In the Vedic verses, we find constant mention of conflicts between the original inhabitants of Ancient India and the colonists. There we find the expression of a spirit that was one of mutual distrust, and a struggle in which was sought either wholesale slavery or extermination for the opponents carried on in the manner of animals who live in the narrow segregation imposed upon them by their limited imagination and imperfect sympathy. This spirit would have continued in all its ferocious vigour of savagery had men failed to find the opportunity for the discovery that man's highest truth was in the union of co-operation and love.

The progress of agriculture was the first external step which led to such a discovery. It not only made a settled life possible for a large number of men living in close proximity, but it claimed for its very purpose a life of peaceful co-operation. The mere fact of such a sudden change from a nomadic to an agricultural condition would not have benefited man if he had not developed therewith his spiritual sensitiveness to an inner principle of truth. We can realize, from our reading of the Ramayana, the birth of idealism among a section of the Indian colonists of those days, before whose mind's eye was opened a vision of emancipation rich with the responsibility of a higher life. The epic represents in its ideal the change of the people's aspiration from the path of conquest to that of reconciliation.

At the present time, as I have said, the human world has been overtaken by another vast change similar to that which had occurred in the epic age of India. So long men had been cultivating, almost with a religious fervour, that mentality which is the product of racial isolation; poets proclaimed, in a loud

117

pitch of bragging, the exploits of their popular fighters; money makers felt neither pity nor shame in the unscrupulous dexterity of their pocket-picking; diplomats scattered lies in order to reap concessions from the devastated future of their own victims. Suddenly the walls that separated the different races are seen to have given way, and we find ourselves standing face to face.

This is a great fact of epic significance. Man, suckled at the wolf's breasts, sheltered in the brute's den, brought up in the prowling habit of depredation, suddenly discovers that he is Man, and that his true power lies in yielding up his brute power for the freedom of spirit.

The God of humanity has arrived at the gates of the ruined temple of the tribe. Though he has not yet found his altar, I ask the men of simple faith, wherever they may be in the world, to bring their offering of sacrifice to him, and to believe that it is far better to be wise and worshipful than to be clever and supercilious. I ask them to claim the right of manhood to be friends of men, and not the right of a particular proud race or nation which may boast of the fatal quality of being the rulers of men. We should know for certain that such rulers will no longer be tolerated in the new world, as it basks in the open sunlight of mind and breathes life's free air.

In the geological ages of the infant earth the demons of physical force had their full sway. The angry fire, the devouring flood, the fury of the storm, continually kicked the earth into frightful distortions. These titans have at last given way to the reign of life. Had there been spectators in those days who were clever and practical they would have wagered their last penny on these titans and would have waxed hilariously witty at the expense of the helpless living speck taking its stand in the arena of the wrestling giants. Only a dreamer could have then declared with unwavering conviction that those titans were doomed because of their very exaggeration, as are, to-day, those formidable qualities which, in the parlance of schoolboy science, are termed Nordic.

I ask once again, let us, the dreamers of the East and the West, keep our faith firm in the Life that creates and not in the Machine that constructs in the power that hides its force and blossoms in beauty, and not in the power that bares its arms and chuckles at its capacity to make itself obnoxious. Let us know that the Machine is good when it helps, but not so when it exploits life; that Science is great when it destroys evil, but not when the two enter into unholy alliance.

Chapter XII

The Teacher

I have already described how the nebulous idea of the divine essence condensed in my consciousness into a human realization. It is definite and finite at the same time, the Eternal Person manifested in all persons. It may be one of the numerous manifestations of God, the one in which is comprehended Man and his Universe. But we can never know or imagine him as revealed in any other inconceivable universe so long as we remain human beings. And therefore, whatever character our theology may ascribe to him, in reality he is the infinite ideal of Man towards whom men move in their collective growth, with whom they seek their union of love as individuals, in whom they find their ideal of father, friend and beloved.

I am sure that it was this idea of the divine Humanity unconsciously working in my mind, which compelled me to come out of the seclusion of my literary career and take my part in the world of practical activities. The solitary enjoyment of the infinite in meditation no longer satisfied me, and the texts which I used for my silent worship lost their inspiration without my knowing it. I am sure I vaguely felt that my need was spiritual self-realization in the life of Man through some disinterested service. This was the time when I founded an educational institution for our children in Bengal. It has a special character of its own which is still struggling to find its fulfilment; for it is a living temple that I have attempted to build for my divinity. In such a place education necessarily becomes the preparation for a complete life of man which can only become possible by living that life, through knowledge and service, enjoyment and creative work. The necessity was my own, for I felt impelled to come back into a fullness of truth from my exile in a dream-world.

This brings to my mind the name of another poet of ancient India, Kalidasa, whose poem of Meghaduta reverberates with the music of the sorrow of an exile.

It was not the physical home-sickness from which the poet suffered, it was something far more fundamental, the home-sickness of the soul. We feel from almost all his works the oppressive atmosphere of the kings' palaces of those days, dense with things of luxury, and also with the callousness of self-indulgence, albeit an atmosphere of refined culture based on an extravagant civilization.

The poet in the royal court lived in banishment—banishment from the immediate presence of the eternal. He knew it was not merely his own banishment, but that of the whole age to which he was born, the age that had gathered its wealth and missed its well-being, built its storehouse of things and lost its background of the great universe. What was the form in which his desire for perfection persistently appeared in his drama and poems? It was the form of the *tapovana*, the forest-dwelling of the patriarchal community of ancient India. Those who are familiar with Sanskrit literature will know that this was not a colony of people with a primitive culture and mind. They were seekers after truth, for the sake of which they lived in an atmosphere of purity but not of Puritanism, of the simple life but not the life of self-mortification. They never advocated celibacy and they had constant inter-communication with other people who lived the life of worldly interest. Their aim and endeavour have briefly been suggested in the Upanishad in these lines:

Te sarvagam sarvatah prapya dhira
yuktatmanah sarvamevavisanti.

(Those men of serene mind enter into the All, having realized and being in union everywhere with the omnipresent Spirit.)

It was never a philosophy of renunciation of a negative character, but a realization completely comprehensive. How the tortured mind of Kalidasa in the prosperous city of Ujjaini, and the glorious period of Vikramaditya, closely pressed by all-obstructing things and all-devouring self, let his thoughts hover round the vision of a *tapovana* for his inspiration of life!

It was not a deliberate copy but a natural coincidence that a poet of modern India also had the similar vision when he felt within him the misery of a spiritual banishment. In the time of Kalidasa the people vividly believed in the ideal of *tapovana*, the forest colony, and there can be no doubt that even in the late age there were communities of men living in the heart of nature, not ascetics fiercely in love with a lingering suicide, but men of serene sanity who sought to realize the spiritual meaning of their life. And, therefore, when Kalidasa sang of the *tapovana*, his poems found their immediate communion in the living faith of his hearers. But to-day the idea has lost any definite outline of reality, and has retreated into the far-away phantom-land of legend. Therefore the Sanskrit word in a modern poem would merely be poetical, its meaning judged by a literary standard of appraisement. Then, again, the spirit of the forest-dwelling in the purity of its original shape would be a fantastic anachronism in the present age, and therefore, in order to be real, it must find its reincarnation under modern conditions of life. It must be the same in truth, but not identical in fact. It was this which made the modern poet's heart crave to compose his poem in a language of tangible words.

But I must give the history in some detail. Civilized man has come far away from the orbit of his normal life. He has gradually formed and intensified some habits that are like those of the bees for adapting himself to his hive-world. We often see men suffering from ennui, from world-weariness, from a spirit of rebellion against their environment for no reasonable cause whatever. Social revolutions are constantly ushered in with a suicidal violence that has its origin in our dissatisfaction with our hive-wall arrangement—the too exclusive enclosure that deprives us of the perspective which is so much needed to give us the proper proportion in our art of living. All this is an indication that man has not been moulded on the model of the bee and therefore he becomes recklessly antisocial when his freedom to be more than social is ignored.

In our highly complex modern condition mechanical forces are organized with such efficiency that materials are produced that grow far in advance of man's selective and assimilative capacity to simplify them into harmony with his nature and needs.

Such an intemperate overgrowth of things, like rank vegetation in the tropics, creates confinement for man. The nest is simple, it has an early relationship with the sky; the cage is complex and costly; it is too much itself excommunicated from whatever lies outside. And man is building his cage, fast developing his parasitism on the monster Thing, which he allows to envelop him on all sides. He is always occupied in adapting himself to its dead angularities, limits himself to its limitations, and merely becomes a part of it.

This may seem contrary to the doctrine of those who believe that a constant high pressure of living, produced by an artificially cultivated hunger of things, generates and feeds the energy that drives civilization upon its endless journey. Personally, I do not believe that this has ever been the principal driving force that has led to eminence any great civilization of which we know in history.

I was born in what was once the metropolis of British India. My own ancestors came floating to Calcutta upon the earliest tide of the fluctuating fortune of the East India Company. The unconventional code of life for our family has been a confluence of three cultures, the Hindu, Mohammedan and British. My grandfather belonged to that period when the amplitude of dress and courtesy and a generous leisure were gradually being clipped and curtailed into Victorian manners, economical in time, in ceremonies, and in the dignity of personal appearance. This will show that I came to a world in which the modern city-bred spirit of progress had just begun driving its triumphal car over the luscious green life of our ancient village community. Though the trampling process was almost complete round me, yet the wailing cry of the past was still lingering over the wreckage.

Often I had listened to my eldest brother describing with the poignancy of a hopeless regret a society hospitable, sweet with the old-world aroma of natural kindliness, full of simple faith and the ceremonial-poetry of life. But all this was a vanishing shadow behind me in the dusky golden haze of a twilight horizon—the all-pervading fact around my boyhood being the modern city newly built by a company of western traders and the spirit of the modern time seeking its unaccustomed entrance into our life, stumbling against countless anomalies.

But it always is a surprise to me to think that though this closed-up hardness of a city was my only experience of the world, yet my mind was constantly haunted by the homesick fancies of an exile. It seems that the sub-conscious remembrance of a primeval dwelling-place, where, in our ancestor's minds, were figured and voiced the mysteries of the inarticulate rocks, the rushing water and the dark whispers of the forest, was constantly stirring my blood with its call. Some shadow-haunting living reminiscence in me seemed to ache for the prenatal cradle and playground it shared with the primal life in the illimitable magic of the land, water and air. The shrill, thin cry of the high-flying kite in the blazing sun of the dazed Indian midday sent to a solitary boy the signal of a dumb distant kinship. The few coconut plants growing by the boundary wall of our house, like some war captives from an older army of invaders of this earth, spoke to me of the eternal companionship which the great brotherhood of trees has ever offered to man.

Looking back upon those moments of my boyhood days, when all my mind seemed to float poised upon a large feeling of the sky, of the light, and to tingle with the brown earth in its glistening grass, I cannot help believing that my Indian ancestry had left deep in my being the legacy of its philosophy—the philosophy which speaks of fulfilment through our harmony with all things. The founding of my school had its origin in the memory of that longing for the freedom of consciousness, which seems to go back beyond the skyline of my birth.

Freedom in the mere sense of independence has no content, and therefore no meaning. Perfect freedom lies in a perfect harmony of relationship, which we realize in this world not through our response to it in knowing, but in being. Objects of knowledge maintain an infinite distance from us who are the knowers. For knowledge is not union. Therefore the further world of freedom awaits us there where we reach truth, not through feeling it by our senses or knowing it by our reason, but through the union of perfect sympathy.

Children with the freshness of their senses come directly to the intimacy of this world. This is the first great gift they have. They must accept it naked and simple and must never again lose their power of immediate communication with it. For our perfection we have to be vitally savage and mentally civilized; we should have the gift to be natural with nature and human with human society. My banished soul sitting in the civilized isolation of the town-life cried within me for the enlargement of the horizon of its comprehension. I was like the torn-away line of a verse, always in a state of suspense, while the other line, with which it rhymed and which could give it fullness, was smudged by the mist away in some undecipherable distance. The inexpensive power to be happy, which, along with other children, I brought to this world, was being constantly worn away by friction with the brick-and-mortar arrangement of life, by monotonously mechanical habits and the customary code of respectability.

In the usual course of things I was sent to school, but possibly my suffering was unusually greater than that of most other children. The non-civilized in me was sensitive; it had the great thirst for colour, for music, for movement of life. Our city-built education took no heed of that living fact. It had its luggage-van waiting for branded bales of marketable result. The relative proportion of the non-civilized to the civilized in man should be in the proportion of the water and the land in our globe, the former predominating. But the school had for its object a continual reclamation of the civilized. Such a drain in the fluid element causes an aridity which may not be considered deplorable under city conditions. But my nature never got accustomed to those conditions, to the callous decency of the pavement. The non-civilized triumphed in me only too soon and drove me away from school when I had just entered my teens. I found myself stranded on a solitary island of ignorance, and had to rely solely upon my own instincts to build up my education from the very beginning.

This reminds me that when I was young I had the great good fortune of coming upon a Bengali translation of *Robinson Crusoe*. I still believe that it is the best book for boys that has ever been written. There was a longing in me when young to run away from my own self and be one with everything in Nature. This mood appears to be particularly Indian, the outcome of a traditional desire for the expansion of consciousness. One has to admit that such a desire is too subjective in its character; but this is inevitable in the geographical circumstances which we have to endure. We live under the extortionate tyranny of the tropics, paying heavy toll every moment for the barest right of existence. The heat, the damp, the unspeakable fecundity of minute life feeding upon big life, the perpetual sources of irritation, visible and invisible, leave very little margin of capital for extravagant experiments. Excess of energy seeks obstacles for its self-realization. That is why we find so often in Western literature a constant emphasis upon the malignant aspect of Nature, in whom the people of the West seem to be delighted to discover an enemy for the sheer enjoyment of challenging her to fight. The reason which made Alexander express his desire to find other worlds to conquer, when his conquest of the world was completed, makes the enormously vital people of the West desire, when they have some respite in their sublime mission of fighting against objects that are noxious, to go out of their way to spread their coat-tails in other people's thorough-fares and to claim indemnity when these are trodden upon. In order to make the thrilling risk of hurting themselves they are ready to welcome endless trouble to hurt others who are inoffensive, such as the beautiful birds which happen to know how to fly away, the timid beasts, which have the advantage of inhabiting inaccessible regions, and—but I avoid the discourtesy of mentioning higher races in this connection.

Life's fulfilment finds constant contradictions in its path; but those are necessary for the sake of its advance. The stream is saved from the sluggishness of its current by the perpetual opposition of the soil through which it must cut its way. It is this soil which forms its banks. The spirit of fight belongs to the genius of life. The tuning of an instrument has to be done, not because it reveals a proficient perseverance in the face of difficulty, but because it helps music to be perfectly realized. Let us rejoice that in the West life's instrument is being tuned in all its different chords owing to the great fact that the West has triumphant pleasure in the struggle with obstacles. The spirit of creation in the heart of the universe will never allow, for its own sake, obstacles to be completely removed. It is only because positive truth lies in that ideal of perfection, which has to be won by our own endeavour in order to make it our own, that the spirit of fight is great. But this does not imply a premium for the exhibition of a muscular athleticism or a rude barbarism of ravenous rapacity.

In *Robinson Crusoe*, the delight of the union with Nature finds its expression in a story of adventure in which the solitary Man is face to face with solitary Nature, coaxing her, co-operating with her, exploring her secrets, using all his faculties to win her help.

This is the heroic love-adventure of the West, the active wooing of the earth. I remember how, once in my youth, the feeling of intense delight and wonder followed me in my railway journey across Europe from Brindisi to Calais, when I realized the chaste beauty of this continent everywhere blossoming in a glow of health and richness under the age-long attention of her chivalrous lover, Western humanity. He had gained her, made her his own, unlocked the inexhaustible generosity of her heart. And I had intently wished that the introspective vision of the universal soul, which an Eastern devotee realizes in the solitude of his mind, could be united with this spirit of its outward expression in service, the exercise of will in unfolding the wealth of beauty and well-being from its shy obscurity to the light.

I remember the morning when a beggar woman in a Bengal village gathered in the loose end of her *sari* the stale flowers that were about to be thrown away from the vase on my table; and with an ecstatic expression of tenderness buried her face in them, exclaiming, "Oh, Beloved of my Heart!" Her eyes could easily pierce the veil of the outward form and reach the realm of the infinite in these flowers, where she found the intimate touch of her Beloved, the great, the universal Human. But in spite of it all she lacked that energy of worship, that Western form of direct divine service, the service of man, which helps the earth to bring out her flowers and spread the reign of beauty on the desolate dust. I refuse to think that the twin spirits of the East and the West, the Mary and Martha, can never meet to make perfect the realization of truth. And in spite of our material poverty in the East and the antagonism of time I wait patiently for this meeting.

Robinson Crusoe's island comes to my mind when I think of some institution where the first great lesson in the perfect union of Man and Nature, not only through love, but through active communication and intelligent ways, can be had unobstructed. We have to keep in mind the fact that love and action are the only intermediaries through which perfect knowledge can be obtained; for the object of knowledge is not pedantry but wisdom. The primary object of an institution should not be merely to educate one's limbs and mind to be in efficient readiness for all emergencies, but to be in perfect tune in the symphony of response between life and world, to find the balance of their harmony which is wisdom. The first important lesson for children in such a place would be that of improvization, the constant imposition of the ready-made having been banished from here. It is to give occasions to explore one's capacity through surprises of achievement. I must make it plain that this means a lesson not in simple life, but in creative life. For life may grow complex, and yet if there is a living personality in its centre, it will still have the unity of creation; it will carry its own weight in perfect grace, and will not be a mere addition to the number of facts that only goes to swell a crowd.

I wish I could say that I had fully realized my dream in my school. I have only made the first introduction towards it and have given an opportunity to the children to find their freedom in Nature by being able to love it. For love is freedom; it gives us that fullness of existence which saves us from paying with our soul for objects that are immensely cheap. Love lights up this world with its meaning and makes life feel that it has that "enough" everywhere which truly is its "feast". I know men who preach the cult of simple life by glorifying the spiritual merit of poverty. I refuse to imagine any special value in poverty when it is a mere negation. Only when the mind has the sensitiveness to be able to respond to the deeper call of reality is it naturally weaned away from the lure of the fictitious value of things. It is callousness which robs us of our simple power to enjoy, and dooms us to the indignity of a snobbish pride in furniture and the foolish burden of expensive things. But the callousness of asceticism pitted against the callousness of luxury is merely fighting one evil with the help of another, inviting the pitiless demon of the desert in place of the indiscriminate demon of the jungle.

I tried my best to develop in the children of my school the freshness of their feeling for Nature, a sensitiveness of soul in their relationship with their human surroundings, with the help of literature, festive ceremonials and also the religious teaching which enjoins us to come to the nearer presence of the world through the soul, thus to gain it more than can be measured— like gaining an instrument in truth by bringing out its music.

Chapter XIII

Spiritual Freedom

THERE are injuries that attack our life; they hurt the harmony of life's functions through which is maintained the harmony of our physical self with the physical world; and these injuries are called diseases. There are also factors that oppress our intelligence. They injure the harmony of relationship between our rational mind and the universe of reason; and we call them stupidity, ignorance or insanity. They are uncontrolled exaggerations of passions that upset all balance in our personality. They obscure the harmony between the spirit of the individual man and the spirit of the universal Man; and we give them the name sin. In all these instances our realization of the universal Man, in his physical, rational and spiritual aspects, is obstructed, and our true freedom in the realms of matter, mind and spirit is made narrow or distorted.

All the higher religions of India speak of the training for *Mukti*, the liberation of the soul. In this self of ours we are conscious of individuality, and all its activities are engaged in the expression and enjoyment of our finite and individual nature. In our soul we are conscious of the transcendental truth in us, the Universal, the Supreme Man; and this soul, the spiritual self, has its enjoyment in the renunciation of the individual self for the sake of the supreme soul. This renunciation is not in the negation of self, but in the dedication of it. The desire for it comes from an instinct which very often knows its own meaning vaguely and gropes for a name that would define its purpose. This purpose is in the realization of its unity with some objective ideal of perfections, some harmony of relationship between the individual and the infinite man. It is of this harmony, and not of a barren isolation that the Upanishad speaks, when it says that truth no longer remains hidden in him who finds himself in the All.

Once when I was on a visit to a remote Bengali village, mostly inhabited by Mahomedan cultivators, the villagers entertained me with an operatic performance the literature of which belonged to an obsolete religious sect that had wide influence centuries ago. Though the religion itself is dead, its voice still continues preaching its philosophy to a people who, in spite of their different culture, are not tired of listening. It discussed according to its own doctrine the different elements, material and transcendental, that constitute human personality, comprehending the body, the self and the soul. Then came a dialogue, during the course of which was related the incident of a person who wanted to make a journey to Brindaban, the Garden of Bliss, but was prevented by a watchman who startled him with an accusation of theft. The thieving was proved when it was shown that inside his clothes he was secretly trying to smuggle into the garden the self, which only finds its fulfilment by its surrender. The culprit was caught with the incriminating bundle in his possession which barred for him his passage to the supreme goal. Under a tattered canopy, supported on bamboo poles and lighted by a few smoking kerosene lamps, the village crowd, occasionally interrupted by howls of jackals in the neighbouring paddy fields, attended with untired interest, till the small hours of the morning, the performance of a drama that discussed the ultimate meaning of all things in a seemingly incongruous setting of dance, music and humorous dialogue.

This illustration will show how naturally, in India, poetry and philosophy have walked hand in hand, only because the latter has claimed its right to guide men to the practical path of their life's fulfilment. What is that fulfilment? It is our freedom in truth, which has for its prayer:

Lead us from the unreal to reality.

For *satyam* is *anandam*, the Real is Joy.

In the world of art, our consciousness being freed from the tangle of self interest, we gain an unobstructed vision of unity, the incarnation of the real, which is a joy forever.

As in the world of art, so in the spiritual world, our soul waits for its freedom from the ego to reach that disinterested joy which is the source and goal of creation. It cries for its *mukti*, its freedom in the unity of truth. The idea of *mukti* has affected our lives in India, touched the springs of pure emotions and supplications; for it soars heavenward on the wings of poesy. We constantly hear men of scanty learning and simple faith singing in their prayer to Tara, the Goddess Redeemer:

"For what sin should I be compelled to remain in this dungeon of the world of appearance?"

They are afraid of being alienated from the world of truth,

afraid of perpetual drifting amidst the froth and foam of things, of being tossed about by the tidal waves of pleasure and pain and never reaching the ultimate meaning of life. Of these men, one may be a carter driving his cart to market, another a fisherman plying his net. They may not be prompt with an intelligent answer if they are questioned about the deeper import of the song they sing, but they have no doubt in their mind that the abiding cause of all misery is not so much in the lack of life's furniture as in the obscurity of life's significance. It is a common topic with such to decry an undue emphasis upon "me" and "mine", which falsifies the perspective of truth. For have they not often seen men, who are not above their own level in social position or intellectual acquirement, going out to seek Truth, leaving everything that they have behind them?

They know that the object of these adventurers is not betterment in worldly wealth and power—it is *mukti*, freedom. They possibly know some poor fellow villager of their own craft, who remains in the world carrying on his daily vocation and yet has the reputation of being emancipated in the heart of the Eternal. I myself have come across a fisherman singing with an inward absorption of mind, while fishing all day in the Ganges, who was pointed out to me by my boatman, with awe, as a man of liberated spirit. He is out of reach of the conventional prices that are set upon men by society, and which classify them like toys arranged in the shop-windows according to the market standard of value.

When the figure of this fisherman comes to my mind, I cannot but think that their number is not small who with their lives sing the epic of the unfettered soul, but will never be known in history. These unsophisticated Indian peasants know that an Emperor is merely a decorated slave, remaining chained to his

Empire, that a millionaire is kept pilloried by his fate in the golden cage of his wealth, while this fisherman is free in the realm of light. When, groping in the dark, we stumble against objects, we cling to them believing them to be our only hope. When light comes, we slacken our hold, finding them to be mere parts of the All to which we are related. The simple man of the village knows what freedom is—freedom from the isolation of self, from the isolation of things, which imparts a fierce intensity to our sense of possession. He knows that this freedom is not the mere negation of bondage, in the bareness of our belongings, but in some positive realization which gives pure joy to our being, and he sings: "To him who sinks into the deep, nothing remains unattained." He says again:

> Let my two minds meet and combine,
> And lead me to the city Wonderful.

When that one mind of ours which wanders in search of things in the outer region of the varied, and the other which seeks the inward vision of unity, are no longer in conflict, they help us to realize the *ajab*, the *anirvachaniya*, the ineffable. The poet saint Kabir has also the same message when he sings:

> By saying that Supreme Reality only dwells in the inner realm of spirit, we shame the outer world of matter; and also when we say that he is only in the outside, we do not speak the truth.

According to these singers, truth is in unity, and therefore freedom is in its realization. The texts of our daily worship and meditation are for training our mind to overcome the barrier of separateness from the rest of existence and to realize *advaitam*, the Supreme Unity which is *anantam*, infinitude. It is philosophical wisdom, having its universal radiation in the popular mind in India, that inspires our prayer, our daily spiritual practices. It has its constant urging for us to go beyond the world of appearances, in which facts as facts are alien to us, like the mere sounds of foreign music; it speaks to us of an emancipation in the inner truth of all things, where the endless *Many* reveal the *One*.

Freedom in the material world has also the same meaning expressed in its own language. When nature's phenomena appeared to us as irrelevant, as heterogeneous manifestations of an obscure and irrational caprice, we lived in an alien world never dreaming of our *swaraj* within its territory. Through the discovery of the harmony of its working with that of our reason, we realize our unity with it, and therefore our freedom.

Those who have been brought up in a mis-understanding of this world's process, not knowing that it is one with themselves through the relationship of knowledge and intelligence, are trained as cowards by a hopeless faith in the ordinance of a destiny darkly dealing its blows. They submit without struggle when human rights are denied them, being accustomed to imagine themselves born as outlaws in a world constantly thrusting upon them incomprehensible surprises of accidents.

Also in the social or political field, the lack of freedom is based upon the spirit of alienation, on the imperfect realization of the One. There our bondage is in the tortured link of union. One may imagine that an individual who succeeds in dissociating himself from his fellows attains real freedom, inas-much as all ties of relationship imply obligation to others. But we know that, though it may sound paradoxical, it is true that in the human world only a perfect arrangement of interdependence gives rise to freedom. The most individualistic of human beings who own no responsibility are the savages who fail to attain their fulness of manifestation. They live immersed in obscurity, like an ill-lighted fire that cannot liberate itself from its envelope of smoke. Only those may attain their freedom from the segregation of an eclipsed life who have the power to cultivate mutual understanding and co-operation. The history of the growth of freedom is the history of the perfection of human relationship.

It has become possible for men to say that existence is evil, only because in our blindness we have missed something wherein our existence has its truth. If a bird tries to soar with only one of its wings, it is offended with the wind for buffeting it down to the dust. All broken truths are evil. They hurt because they suggest something they do not offer. Death does not hurt us, but disease does, because disease constantly reminds us of health and yet withholds it from us. And life in a half-world is evil because it feigns finality when it is obviously incomplete, giving us the cup but not the draught of life. All tragedies result from truth remaining a fragment, its cycle not being completed. That cycle finds its end when the individual realizes the universal and thus reaches freedom.

But because this freedom is in truth itself and not in an appearance of it, no hurried path of success, forcibly cut out by the greed of result, can be a true path. And an obscure village poet, unknown to the world of recognized respectability, sings:

> O cruel man of urgent need, must you scorch with
> fire the mind which still is a bud? You will burst
> it into bits, destroy its perfume in your impatience.

138

Do you not see that my Lord, the Supreme Teacher, takes ages to perfect the flower and never is in a fury of haste? But because of your terrible greed, you only rely on force, and what hope is there for you, O man of urgent need? "Prithi", says Madan the poet, "hurt not the mind of my Teacher. Know that only he who follows the simple current and loses himself, can hear the voice. O man of urgent need."

This poet knows that there is no external means of taking freedom by the throat. It is the inward process of losing ourselves that leads to it. Bondage in all its forms has its stronghold in the inner self and not in the outside world; it is in the dimming of our consciousness, in the narrowing of our perspective, in the wrong valuation of things.

Let me conclude this chapter with a song of the Baül sect in Bengal, over a century old, in which the poet sings of the eternal bond of union between the infinite and the finite soul, from which there can he no *mukti*, because love is ultimate, because it is an inter-relation which makes truth complete, because absolute independence is the blankness of utter servility. The song runs thus:

It goes on blossoming for ages, the soul-lotus, in which I am bound, as well as thou, without escape. There is no end to the opening of its petals, and the honey in it has so much sweetness that thou, like an enchanted bee, canst never desert it, and therefore thou art bound, and I am, and *mukti* is nowhere.

Chapter XIV

The Four Stages of Life

I have expressly said that I have concentrated my attention upon the subject of religion which is solely related to man, helping him to train his attitude and behaviour towards the infinite in its human aspect. At the same time it should be understood that the tendency of the Indian mind has ever been towards that transcendentalism which does not hold religion to be ultimate but rather to be a means to a further end. This end consists in the perfect liberation of the individual in the universal spirit across the furthest limits of humanity itself.

Such an extreme form of mysticism may be explained to my Western readers by its analogy in science. For science may truly be described as mysticism in the realm of material knowledge. It helps us to go beyond appearances and reach the inner reality of things in principles which are abstractions; it emancipates our mind from the thraldom of the senses to the freedom of reason.

The common-sense view of the world that is apparent to us has its vital importance for ourselves. For all our practical purposes the earth *is* flat, the sun *does* set behind the western horizon; and whatever may be the verdict of the great mathematician about the lack of consistency in time's dealings we should fully trust it in setting our watches right. In questions relating to the arts and our ordinary daily avocations we must treat material objects as they seem to be and not as they are in essence. But the revelations of science, even when they go far beyond man's power of direct perception, give him the purest feeling of disinterested delight and a supersensual background to his world. Science offers us the mystic knowledge of matter which very often passes the range of our imagination. We humbly accept it, following those teachers who have trained their reason to free itself from the trammels of appearance or personal preferences. Their mind dwells in an impersonal infinity where there is no distinction between good and bad, high and low, ugly and beautiful, useful and useless, where all things have their one common right of recognition, that of their existence.

The final freedom of spirit which India aspires after has a similar character of realization. It is beyond all limits of personality, divested of all moral or aesthetic distinctions; it is the pure consciousness of Being, the ultimate reality, which has an infinite illumination of bliss. Though science brings our thoughts to the utmost limit of mind's territory it cannot transcend its own creation made of a harmony of logical symbols. In it the chick has come out of its shell, but not out of the definition of its own chickenhood. But in India it has been said by the *yogi* that through an intensive process of concentration and quietude our consciousness *does* reach that infinity where knowledge ceases to be knowledge, subject and object become one—a state of existence that cannot be defined.

We have our personal self. It has its desires which struggle to create a world where they could have their unrestricted activity and satisfaction. While it goes on we discover that our self-realization reaches its perfection in the abnegation of self. This fact has made us aware that the individual finds his meaning in a fundamental reality comprehending all individuals—the reality which is the moral and spiritual basis of the realm of human values. This belongs to our religion. As science is the liberation of our knowledge in the universal reason, which cannot be other than human reason, religion is the liberation of our individual personality in the universal Person who is human all the same.

The ancient explorers in psychology in India who declare that our emancipation can be carried still further into a realm where infinity is not bounded by human limitations, are not content with advancing this as a doctrine; they advocate its pursuit for the attainment of the highest goal of man. And for its sake the path of discipline has been planned which should be opened out across our life through all its stages, helping us to develop our humanity to perfection, so that we may surpass it in a finality of freedom.

Perfection has its two aspects in man which can to some extent be separated, the perfection in being and perfection in doing. It can be imagined that, through some training or compulsion, good works may possibly be extorted from a man who personally may not be good. Activities that have fatal risks are often undertaken by cowards even though they are conscious of the danger. Such works may be useful and may continue to exist beyond the lifetime of the individual who produced them. And yet, where the question is not that of utility but of moral perfection, we hold it important that the individual should be true in his goodness. His outer good work may continue to produce good results, but the inner perfection of his personality has its own immense value, which for him is spiritual freedom and for humanity is an endless asset though we may not know it. For goodness represents the detachment of our spirit from the exclusiveness of our egoism; in goodness we identify ourselves with the universal humanity. Its value is not merely in some benefit for our fellow beings, but in its truth itself through which we realize within us that man is not merely an animal, bound by his individual passions and appetites, but a spirit that has its unfettered perfection. Goodness is the freedom of our self in the world of man, as is love. We have to be true within, not for worldly duties, but for that spiritual fulfilment, which is in harmony with the Perfect, in union with the Eternal. If this were not true, then mechanical perfection would be considered to be of higher value than the spiritual. In order to realize his unity with the universal, the individual man must live his perfect life which alone gives him the freedom to transcend it.

Doubtless Nature, for its own biological purposes, has created in us a strong faith in life, by keeping us unmindful of death. Nevertheless, not only our physical existence, but also the environment which it builds up around itself, may desert us in the moment of triumph; the greatest prosperity comes to its end, dissolving into emptiness; the mightiest empire is overtaken by stupor amidst the flicker of its festival lights. All this is none the less true because its truism bores us to be reminded of it.

And yet it is equally true that, though all our mortal relationships have their end, we cannot ignore them with impunity while they last. If we behave as if they do not exist, merely because they will not continue for ever, they will all the same exact their dues, with a great deal over by way of penalty. Trying to ignore bonds that are real, albeit temporary, only strengthens and prolongs their bondage. The soul is great, but the self has to be crossed over in order to reach it. We do not attain our goal by destroying our path.

Our teachers in ancient India realized the soul of man as something very great indeed. They saw no end to its dignity, which found its consummation in Brahma himself. Any limited view of man would therefore be an incomplete view. He could not reach his finality as a mere Citizen or Patriot, for neither City nor Country, nor the bubble called the World, could contain his eternal soul.

Bhartrihari, who was once a king, has said: "What if you have secured the fountainhead of all desires; what if you have put your foot on the neck of your enemy, or by your good fortune gathered friends around you? What, even, if you have succeeded in keeping mortal bodies alive for ages—*tatah kim*, what then?"

That is to say, man is greater than all these objects of his desire. He is true in his freedom.

But in the process of attaining freedom one must bind his will in order to save its forces from distraction and wastage, so as to gain for it the velocity which comes from the bondage itself. Those also, who seek liberty in a purely political plane, constantly curtail it and reduce their freedom of thought and action to that narrow limit which is necessary for making political power secure, very often at the cost of liberty of conscience.

India had originally accepted the bonds of her social system in order to transcend society, as the rider puts reins on his horse and stirrups on his own feet in order to ensure greater speed towards his goal.

The Universe cannot be so madly conceived that desire should be an interminable song with no finale. And just as it is painful to stop in the middle of the tune, it should be as pleasant to reach its final cadence.

India has not advised us to come to a sudden stop while work is in full swing. It is true that the unending procession of the world has gone on, through its ups and downs, from the beginning of creation till today; but it is equally obvious that each individual's connection therewith *does* get finished. Must he necessarily quit it without any sense of fulfilment?

So, in the division of man's world-life which we had in India, work came in the middle, and freedom at the end. As the day is divided into morning, noon, afternoon and evening, so India had divided man's life into four parts, following the requirements of his nature. The day has the waxing and waning of its light; so has man the waxing and waning of his bodily powers. Acknowledging this, India gave a connected meaning to his life from start to finish.

First came *brahmacharya*, the period of discipline in education; then *garhasthya*, that of the world's work; then *vanaprasthya*, the retreat for the loosening of bonds; and finally *pravrajya*, the expectant awaiting of freedom across death.

We have come to look upon life as a conflict with death—the intruding enemy, not the natural ending—in impotent quarrel with which we spend every stage of it. When the time comes for youth to depart, we would hold it back by main force. When the fervour of desire slackens, we would revive it with fresh fuel of our own devising. When our sense organs weaken, we urge them to keep up their efforts. Even when our grip has relaxed we are reluctant to give up possession. We are not trained to recognize the inevitable as natural, and so cannot give up gracefully that which has to go, but needs must wait till it is snatched from

145

us. The truth comes as conqueror only because we have lost the art of receiving it as guest.

The stem of the ripening fruit becomes loose, its pulp soft, but its seed hardens with provision for the next life. Our outward losses, due to age, have likewise corresponding inward gains. But, in man's inner life, his will plays a dominant part, so that these gains depend on his own disciplined striving; that is why, in the case of undisciplined man, who has omitted to secure such provision for the next stage, it is so often seen that his hair is grey, his mouth toothless, his muscles slack, and yet his stem-hold on life has refused to let go its grip, so much so that he is anxious to exercise his will in regard to worldly details even after death.

But renounce we must, and through renunciation gain—that is the truth of the inner world.

The flower must shed its petals for the sake of fruition, the fruit must drop off for the re-birth of the tree. The child leaves the refuge of the womb in order to achieve the further growth of body and mind in which consists the whole of the child life; next, the soul has to come out of this self-contained stage into the fuller life, which has varied relations with kinsman and neighbour, together with whom it forms a larger body; lastly comes the decline of the body, the weakening of desire. Enriched with its experiences, the soul now leaves the narrower life for the universal life, to which it dedicates its accumulated wisdom and itself enters into relations with the Life Eternal, so that, when finally the decaying body has come to the very end of its tether, the soul views its breaking away quite simply and without regret, in the expectation of its own entry into the Infinite.

From individual body to community, from community to

universe, from universe to Infinity—this is the soul's normal progress.

Our teachers, therefore, keeping in mind the goal of this progress, did not, in life's first stage of education, prescribe merely the learning of books or things, but *brahmacharya*, the living in discipline, whereby both enjoyment and its renunciation would come with equal ease to the strengthened character. Life being a pilgrimage, with liberation in Brahma as its object, the living of it was as a spiritual exercise to be carried through its different stages, reverently and with a vigilant determination. And the pupil, from his very initiation, had this final consummation always kept in his view.

Once the mind refuses to be bound by temperate requirements, there ceases to be any reason why it should cry halt at any particular limit; and so, like trying to extinguish fire with oil, its acquisitions only make its desires blaze up all the fiercer. That is why it is so essential to habituate the mind, from the very beginning, to be conscious of, and desirous of, keeping within the natural limits; to cultivate the spirit of enjoyment which is allied with the spirit of freedom, the readiness for renunciation.

After the period of such training comes the period of world-life—the life of the householder. Manu tells us:

> It is not possible to discipline ourselves so effectively
> if out of touch with the world, as while pursuing the
> world-life with wisdom.

That is to say, wisdom does not attain completeness except through the living of life; and discipline divorced from wisdom is not true discipline, but merely the meaningless following of custom, which is only a disguise for stupidity.

Work, especially good work, becomes easy only when desire has learnt to discipline itself. Then alone does the house-holder's state become a centre of welfare for all the world, and instead of being an obstacle, helps on the final liberation.

The second stage of life having been thus spent, the decline of the bodily powers must be taken as a warning that it is coming to its natural end. This must not be taken dismally as a notice of dismissal to one still eager to stick to his post, but joyfully as maturity may be accepted as the stage of fulfilment.

After the infant leaves the womb, it still has to remain close to its mother for a time, remaining attached in spite of its detachment, until it can adapt itself to its new freedom. Such is the case in the third stage of life, when man though aloof from the world still remains in touch with it while preparing himself for the final stage of complete freedom. He still gives to the world from his store of wisdom and accepts its support; but this interchange is not of the same intimate character as in the stage of the householder, there being a new sense of distance.

Then at last comes a day when even such free relations have their end, and the emancipated soul steps out of all bonds to face the Supreme Soul.

Only in this way can man's world-life be truly lived from one end to the other, without being engaged at every step in trying conclusions with death, not being overcome, when death comes in due course, as by a conquering enemy.

For this fourfold way of life India attunes man to the grand harmony of the universal, leaving no room for untrained desires of a rampant individualism to pursue their destructive career unchecked, but leading them on to their ultimate modulation in the Supreme.

If we really believe this, then we must uphold an ideal of life in which everything else—the display of individual power, the might of nations—must be counted as subordinate and the soul of man must triumph and liberate itself from the bond of personality which keeps it in an ever-revolving circle of limitation.

If that is not to be, *tatah kim*, what then?

But such an ideal of the utter extinction of the individual separateness has not a universal sanction in India. There are many of us whose prayer is for dualism, so that for them the bond of devotion with God may continue for ever. For them religion is a truth which is ultimate and they refuse to envy those who are ready to sail for the further shore of existence across humanity. They know that human imperfection is the cause of our sorrow, but there is a fulfilment in love with in the range of our limitation which accepts all sufferings and yet rises above them.

Chapter XV

Conclusion

IN the Sanskrit Language the bird is described as "twice-born"—once in its limited shell and then finally in the freedom of the unbounded sky. Those of our community who believe in the liberation of man's limited self in the freedom of the spirit retain the same epithet for themselves. In all departments of life man shows this dualism—his existence within the range of obvious facts and his transcendence of it in a realm of deeper meaning.

Having this instinct inherent in his mind which ever suggests to him the crossing of the border, he has never accepted what is apparent as final, and his incessant struggle has been to break through the shell of his limitations. In this attempt he often goes against the instincts of his vital nature, and even exults in his defiance of the extreme penal laws of the biological kingdom. The best wealth of his civilization has been achieved by his following the guidance of this instinct in his ceaseless adventure of the Endless Further. His achievement of truth goes far beyond his needs and the realization of his self strives across the frontier of its individual interest. This proves to him his infinity and makes his religion real to him by his own manifestation in truth and goodness. Only for man there can be religion because his evolution is from efficiency in nature towards the perfection of spirit.

According to some interpretations of the Vedanta doctrine Brahman is the absolute Truth, the impersonal It, in which there can be no distinction of this and that, the good and the evil, the beautiful and its opposite, having no other quality except its ineffable blissfulness in the eternal solitude of its consciousness utterly devoid of all things and all thoughts. But as our religion can only have its significance in this phenomenal world comprehended by our human self, this absolute conception of Brahman is outside the subject of my discussion. What I have tried to bring out in this book is the fact that whatever name may have been given to the divine Reality it has found its highest place in the history of our religion owing to its human character, giving meaning to the idea of sin and sanctity, and offering an eternal background to all the ideals of perfection which have their harmony with man's own nature.

We have the age-long tradition in our country, as I have already stated, that through the process of *yoga* man can transcend the utmost bounds of his humanity and find himself in a pure state of consciousness of his undivided unity with Parabrahman. There is none who has the right to contradict this belief; for it is a matter of direct experience and not of logic. It is widely known in India that there are individuals who have the power to attain temporarily the state of *Samadhi*, the complete merging of the self in the infinite, a state which is indescribable. While accepting their testimony as true, let us at the same time have faith in the testimony of others who have felt a profound love, which is the intense feeling of union, for a Being who comprehends in himself all things that are human in knowledge, will and action. And he is God, who is not merely a sum total of facts, but the goal that lies immensely beyond all that is comprised in the past and the present.

Appendices

The Baül Singers of Bengal

THE following account of the Baüls in Northern India has been given in the *Visvabharati Quarterly* by my friend and fellow-worker, Professor Kshiti Mohun Sen of Santiniketan, to whom I am grateful for having kindly allowed me to reproduce what he has written in this Appendix:

Baül means madcap, from *bayu* (Skt. Vayu) in its sense of nerve current, and has become the appellation of a set of people who do not conform to established social usage. This derivation is supported by the following verse of Narahari:

"That is why, brother, I became a madcap Baül.
No master I obey, nor injunctions, canons or custom.
Now no men-made distinctions have any hold on
  me,
And I revel only in the gladness of my own welling
  love.

In love there's no separation, but commingling
always.
So I rejoice in song and dance with each and all."

These lines also introduce us to the main tenets of the cult. The freedom, however, that the Baüls seek from all forms of outward compulsion goes even further, for among such are recognized as well the compulsions exerted by our desires and antipathies. Therefore, according to this cult, in order to gain real freedom, one has first to die to the life of the world whilst still in the flesh—for only then can one be rid of all extraneous claims. Those of the Baüls who have Islamic leanings call such "death in life" *fana*, a term used by the Sufis to denote union with the Supreme Being. True love, according to the Baüls, is incompatible with any kind of compulsion. Unless the bonds of necessity are overcome, liberation is out of the question. Love represents the wealth of life which is in excess of need.... From hard, practical politics touching our earth to the nebulous regions of abstract metaphysics, everywhere India expressed the power of her genius equally well.... And yet none of these, neither severally nor collectively, constituted her specific genius; none showed the full height to which she could raise herself, none compassed the veritable amplitude of her innermost reality. It is when we come to the domain of the Spirit, of God-realization, that we find the real nature and stature and genius of the Indian people; it is here that India lives and moves as in her own home of Truth.

The Baül cult is followed by householders as well as homeless wanderers, neither of whom acknowledge class or caste, special deities, temples or sacred places. Though they congregate on the occasion of religious festivals, mainly of the Vaishnavas, held in special centres, they never enter any temple. They do not set up any images of divinities, or religious symbols, in their own places of worship or mystic realization. True, they sometimes maintain with care and reverence spots sacred to some esteemed master or devotee, but they perform no worship there. Devotees from the lowest strata of the Hindu and Moslem communities are welcomed into their ranks, hence the Baüls are looked down upon by both. It is possible that their own contempt for temples had its origin in the denial of admittance therein to their low class brethren. What need, say they, have we of other temples, is not this body of ours the temple where the Supreme Spirit has His abode? The human body, despised by most other religions, is thus for them the holy of holies, wherein the Divine is intimately enshrined as the Man of the Heart. And in this wise is the dignity of Man upheld by them.

Kabir, Nanak, Ravidas, Dadu and his followers have also called man's body the temple of God—the microcosm in which the cosmic abode of the all-pervading Supreme Being is represented.

Kabir says:

"In this body is the Garden of Paradise; herein are comprised the seven seas and the myriad stars; here is the Creator manifest." (I. 101.)

Dadu says:

"This body is my scripture; herein the All-Merciful has written for me His message."

Rajjab (Dadu's chief Moslem disciple) says:

> "Within the devotee is the paper on which the
> scriptures are written in letters of Life. But few care
> to read them; they turn a deaf ear to the message of
> the heart."

Most Indian sects adopt some distinct way of keeping the hair of head and face as a sign of their sect or order. Therefore, so as to avoid being dragged into any such distinctions, the Baüls allow hair and beard and moustache to grow freely. Thus do we remain simple, they say. The similar practice of the Sikhs in this matter is to be noted. Neither do the Baüls believe that lack of clothing or bareness of body conduce to religious merit. According to them the whole body should be kept decently covered. Hence their long robe, for which, if they cannot afford a new piece of cloth, they gather rags and make it of patches. In this they are different from the ascetic *sanyasins*, but resemble rather the Buddhist monks.

The Baüls do not believe in aloofness from, or renunciation of, any person or thing; their central idea is *yoga*, attachment to and communion with the divine and its manifestations, as the means of realization. We fail to recognize the temple of God in the bodily life of man, they explain, because its lamp is not alight. The true vision must be attained in which this temple will become manifest in each and every human body, where-upon mutual communion and worship will spontaneously arise. Truth cannot be communicated to those on whom you look down. You must be able to see the divine light that shines within them, for it is your own lack of vision that makes all seem dark.

Kabir says the same thing:

> "In every abode the light doth shine; it is you who
> are blind that cannot see. When by dint of looking
> and looking you at length can discern it, the veils of
> this world will be torn asunder." (II. 33.)

> "It is because the devotee is not in communion that
> he says the goal is far away." (II.34.)

Many such similarities are to be observed between the sayings of the Baüls and those of the Upper Indian devotees of the Middle Ages, but, unlike the case of the followers of the latter, the Baüls did not become crystallized into any particular order or religious organization. So, in the Baüls of Bengal, there is to be found a freedom and independence of mind and spirit that resists all attempt at definition. Their songs are unique in courage and felicity of expression. But under modern conditions they are becoming extinct, or at best holding on to external features bereft of their original speciality. It would be a great pity if no record of their achievements should be kept before their culture is lost to the world.

Though the Baüls count amongst their following a variety of sects and castes, both Hindu and Moslem, chiefly coming from the lower social ranks, they refuse to give any other account of themselves to the questioner than that they are Baüls. They acknowledge none of the social or religious formalities, but delight in the ever-changing play of life, which cannot be expressed in mere words but of which something may be captured in song, through the ineffable medium of rhythm and tune.

Their songs are passed on from Master to disciple, the latter when competent adding others of his own, but, as already mentioned, they are never recorded in book form. Their replies to questions are usually given by singing appropriate selections from these songs. If asked the reason why, they say: "We are like birds. We do not walk on our legs, but fly with our wings."

There was a Brahmin of Bikrampur, known as Chhaku Thakur, who was the disciple of a Baül of the Namasudra caste (accounted one of the lowest) and hence had lost his place in his own community. When admonished to be careful about what he uttered, so as to avoid popular odium, he answered with the song:

"Let them relieve their minds by saying what they will,
I pursue my own simple way, fearing none at all.
The Mango seed will continue to produce Mango
    trees, no Jambolans.
This seed of mine will produce the real *me*—all
    glory to my Master!"

Love being the main principle according to the Baüls, a Vaishnava once asked a Baül devotee whether he was aware of the different kinds of love as classified in the Vaishnava scriptures. "What should an illiterate ignoramus like me know of the scriptures?" was the reply. The Vaishnava then offered to read and explain the text, which he proceeded to do, while the Baül listened with such patience as he could muster. When asked for his opinion, after the reading was over, he sang:

"A goldsmith, methinks, has come into the flower
    garden.
He would appraise the lotus, forsooth,
By rubbing it on his touchstone!"

Recruits from the higher castes are rare amongst the Baüls. When any such do happen to come, they are reduced to the level of the rest. Are the lower planks of a boat of any lesser importance than the upper? say they.

Once in Vikrampur, I was seated on the river bank by the side of a Baül. "Father," I asked him, "why is it that you keep no historical record of yourselves for the use of posterity?" "We follow the *sahaj* (simple) way," he replied, "and so leave no trace behind us." The tide had then ebbed, and there was but little water in the river bed.

Only a few boatmen were to be seen pushing their boats along the mud. The Baül continued: "Do the boats that sail over the flooded river leave any mark? What should these boatmen of the muddy track, urged on by their need, know of the *sahaj* (simple) way? The true endeavour is to keep oneself simply afloat in the stream of devotion that flows through the lives of devotees—to mingle one's own devotion with theirs. There are many classes of men amongst the Baüls, but they are all Baüls—they have no other achievement or history. All the streams that fall into the Ganges become the Ganges. So must we lose ourselves in the common stream, else will it cease to be living."

On another Baül being asked why they did not follow the scriptures, "Are we dogs", he replied, "that we should lick up the leavings of others? Brave men rejoice in the output of their own energy, they create their own festivals. These cowards who have not the power to rejoice in themselves have to rely on what others have left. Afraid lest the world should lack festivals in the future, they save up the scraps left over by their predecessors for later use. They are content with glorifying their forefathers because they know not how to create for themselves."

"If you would know that Man,
Simple must be your endeavour.
To the region of the simple must you fare.
Pursuers of the path of man's own handiwork,
Who follow the crowd, gleaning their false leavings,
What news can they get of the Real?"

It is hardly to be wondered at that people who think thus should have no use for history!

We have already noticed that, like all the followers of the simple way, the Baüls have no faith in specially sacred spots or places of pilgrimage, but that they nevertheless congregate on the occasion of religious festivals. If asked why, the Baül says:

"We would be within hail of the other Boatmen, to
    hear their calls,
That we may make sure our boat rightly floats on
    the *sahaj* stream."

Not what men have said or done in the past, but the living human touch is what they find helpful. Here is a song giving their ideas about pilgrimage:

"I would not go, my heart, to Mecca or Medina,
For behold, I ever abide by the side of my Friend.
Mad would I become, had I dwelt afar, not knowing
    Him.
There's no worship in Mosque or Temple or special
    holy day.
At every step I have my Mecca and Kashi; sacred is
    every moment."

If a Baül is asked the age of his cult, whether it comes before or after this one or that, he says, "Only the artificial religions of the world are limited by time. Our *sahaj* (simple, natural) religion is timeless, it has neither beginning nor end, it is of all time." The religion of the Upanishads and Puranas, even that of the Vedas, is, according to them, artificial.

The followers of the *sahaj* cult believe only in living religious experience. Truth, according to them, has two aspects, inert and living. Confined to itself truth has no value for man. It becomes priceless when embodied in a living personality. The conversion of the inert into living truth by the devotee they compare to the conversion into milk by the cow of its fodder, or the conversion by the tree of dead matter into fruit. He who has this power of making truth living, is the Guru or Master. Such Gurus they hold in special reverence, for the eternal and all-pervading truth can only be brought to man's door by passing through his life.

The Baüls say that emptiness of time and space is required for a playground. That is why God has preserved an emptiness in the heart of man, for the sake of His own play of Love. Our wise and learned ones were content with finding in Brahma the *tat* (lit. "that"—the ultimate substance). The Baüls, not being Pandits, do not profess to understand all this fuss about *thatness*, they want a Person. So their God is the Man of the Heart (*manner manush*) sometimes simply the Man (*purush*). This Man of the Heart is ever and anon lost in the turmoil of things. Whilst He is revealed within, no worldly pleasures can give satisfaction. Their sole anxiety is the finding of this Man.

The Baül sings:

"Ah, where am I to find Him, the Man of my Heart?
Alas, since I lost Him, I wander in search of Him,
Thro' lands near and far."

The agony of separation from Him cannot be mitigated for them by learning or philosophy:

"Oh, these words and words, my mind would none
    of them,
The Supreme Man it must and shall discover.
So long as Him I do not see, these mists slake not
    my thirst.
Mad am I; for lack of that Man I madly run about;
For his sake the world I've left; for Bisha naught
    else will serve."

This Bisha was a *bhuin-mali*, by caste, disciple of Bala, the Kaivarta.

This cult of the Supreme Man is only to be found in the Vedas hidden away in the Purusha-sukta (A. V. 19.6). It is more freely expressed by the Upper Indian devotees of the Middle Ages. It is all in all with the Baüls. The God whom these illiterate outcastes seek so simply and naturally in their lives is obscured by the accredited religious leaders in philosophical systems and terminology, in priestcraft and ceremonial, in institutions and temples.

Not satisfied with the *avatars* (incarnations of God) mentioned in the scriptures, the Baül sings:

"As we look on every creature, we find each to be
    His *avatar*.

What can you teach us of His ways? In ever-new play He wondrously revels."

And Kabir also tells us:

"All see the Eternal One, but only the devotee, in his solitude, recognizes him."

A friend of mine was once much impressed by the reply of a Baül who was asked why his robe was not tinted with ascetic ochre:

"Can the colour show outside, unless the inside is first tinctured? Can the fruit attain ripe sweetness by the painting of its skin?"

This aversion of the Baül from outward marks of distinction is also shared by the Upper Indian devotees, as I have elsewhere noticed.

The age-long controversy regarding *dvaita* (dualism) and *advaita* (monism) is readily solved by these wayfarers on the path of Love. Love is the simple striving, love the natural communion, so believe the Baüls. "Ever two and ever one, of this the name of Love", say they. In love, oneness is achieved without any loss of respective selfhood.

The same need exists for the reconcilement of the antagonism between the outer call of the material world and the inner call of the spiritual world, as for the realization of the mutual love of the individual and Supreme self. The God who is Love, say the Baüls, can alone serve to turn the currents of the within and the without in one and the same direction.

Kabir says:

> "If we say He is only within, then the whole Universe
>   is shamed.
> If we say He is only without, then that is false.
> He whose feet rest alike on the sentient and on the
>   inert,
> fills the gap between the inner and the outer world."

The inter-relations of man's body and the Universe have to be realized by spiritual endeavour. Such endeavour is called *Kaya Sadhan* (Realization through the body).

One process in this *Kaya Sadhan* of the Baüls is known as *Urdha-srota* (the elevation of the current). Waters flow downwards according to the ordinary physical law. But with the advent of Life the process is reversed. When the living seed sprouts the juices are drawn upwards, and on the elevation that such flow can attain depends the height of the tree. It is the same in the life of man. His desires ordinarily flow downward towards animality. The endeavour of the expanding spirit is to turn their current upwards towards the light. The currents of *jiva* (animal life) must be converted into the current of *Shiva* (God life). They form a centre round the ego; they must be raised by the force of love.

Says Dadu's daughter, Nanimata:

> "My life is the lamp afloat on the stream.
> To what bourne shall it take me?
> How is the divine to conquer the carnal,

The downward current to be upward turned?
As when the wick is lighted the oil doth upward flow,
So simply is destroyed the thirst of the body."

The *Yoga* Vasistha tells us:

"Uncleansed desires bind to the world, purified desires give liberation."

References to this reversal of current are also to be found in the Atharva Veda (X. 2.9; 2.34). This reversal is otherwise considered by Indian devotees as the conversion of the *sthula* (gross) in the *sukshma* (fine).

The Baül sings:

"Love is my golden touch—it turns desire into service:
Earth seeks to become Heaven, man to become God."

Another aspect of the idea of reversal has been put thus by Rabindranath Tagore in his *Broken Ties*: "If I keep going in the same direction along which He comes to me, then I shall be going further and further away from Him. If I proceed in the opposite direction, then only can we meet. He loves form, so He is continually descending towards form. We cannot live by form alone, so we must ascend towards His formlessness. He is free, so his play is within bonds. We are bound, so we find our joy in freedom. All our sorrow is because we cannot understand this.

He who sings, proceeds from his joy to the tune; he who hears, from the tune to joy. One comes from freedom into bondage, the other goes from bondage into freedom; only thus can they have their communion. He sings and we hear. He ties the bonds as He sings to us, we untie them as we listen to Him."

This idea also occurs in our devotees of the Middle Ages.

The "*sahaj*" folk endeavour to seek the bliss of divine union only for its own sake. Mundane desires are therefore accounted the chief obstacles in the way. But for getting rid of them, the wise Guru, according to the Baüls, does not advise renunciation of the good things of the world, but the opening of the door to the higher self. Thus guided, says Kabir,

> "I close not my eyes, stop not my ears, nor torment
>   my body.
> But every path I then traverse becomes a path of
>   pilgrimage, whatever work I engage in becomes
>   service.
> This simple consummation is the best."

The simple way has led its votaries easily and naturally to their living conception of Humanity.

Rajjab says:

> "All the world is the Veda, all creations the Koran.
>   Why read paper scriptures, O Rajjab?
> Gather ever fresh wisdom from the Universe. The
>   eternal wisdom shines within the concourse of
>   the millions of Humanity."

The Baül sings:

> "The simple has its thirty million strings whose
>   mingled symphony ever sounds.
> Take all the creatures of the World into yourself.
>   Drown yourself in that eternal music."

I conclude with a few more examples of Baül songs, esoteric and otherwise, from amongst many others of equal interest.

By Gangaram, the Namasudra:

> "Realize how finite and unbounded are One,
> As you breathe in and out.
> Of all ages, then, you will count the moments,
> In every moment find the ages,
> The drop in the ocean, the ocean in the drop.
> If your endeavour be but *sahaj*, beyond argument
>   and cogitation,
> You will taste the precious quintessence.
> Blinded are you by over-much journeying from
>   bourne to bourne,
> O Gangaram, be simple! Then alone will vanish all
>   your doubts."

By Bisha, the disciple of Bala:

> "The simple Man was in the Paradise of my heart,
> Alas, how and when did I lose Him,
> That now no peace I know, at home or abroad?

By meditation and telling of beads, in worship and
    travail,
The quest goes on for ever;
But unless the Simple Man comes of Himself,
Fruitless is it all;
For he yields not to forgetfulness of striving.
Bisha's heart has understood right well
That by His own simple way alone is its door
    unlocked."

"Listen, O brother man," declares Chandidas, "the Truth of
Man is the highest of truths; there is no other truth above it."

Appendix II

Note on the Nature of Reality

(A conversation between Rabindranath Tagore and Professor Albert Einstein in the afternoon of July 14, 1930, at the Professor's residence in Kaputh.)

E.: Do you believe in the Divine as isolated from the world?

T: Not isolated. The infinite personality of man comprehends the Universe. There cannot be anything that cannot be subsumed by the human personality, and this proves that the truth of the Universe is human truth. I have taken a scientific fact to illustrate this—Matter is composed of protons and electrons, with gaps between them; but matter may seem to be solid. Similarly humanity is composed of individuals, yet they have their interconnection of human relationship, which gives living solidarity to man's world. The entire universe is linked up with us in a similar manner, it is a human universe. I have pursued this thought through art, literature and the religious consciousness of man.

E.: There are two different conceptions about the nature of

the universe: (1) The world as a unity dependent on humanity. (2) The world as a reality independent of the human factor.

T.: When our universe is in harmony with Man, the eternal, we know it as truth, we feel it as beauty.

E.: This is a purely human conception of the universe.

T.: There can be no other conception. This world is a human world—the scientific view of it is also that of the scientific man. There is some standard of reason and enjoyment which gives it truth, the standard of the Eternal Man whose experiences are through our experiences.

E.: This is a realization of the human entity.

T.: Yes, one eternal entity. We have to realize it through our emotions and activities. We realize the Supreme Man who has no individual limitations through our limitations. Science is concerned with that which is not confined to individuals; it is the impersonal human world of truths. Religion realizes these truths and links them up with our deeper needs; our individual consciousness of truth gains universal significance. Religion applies values to truth, and we know truth as good through our own harmony with it.

E.: Truth, then, or Beauty, is not independent of Man?

T.: No.

E.: If there would be no human beings any more, the Apollo of Belvedere would no longer be beautiful?

T.: No.

E.: I agree with regard to this conception of Beauty, but not with regard to Truth.

T.: Why not? Truth is realized through man.

E.: I cannot prove that my conception is right, but that is my religion.

T.: Beauty is in the ideal of perfect harmony which is in the Universal Being; truth the perfect comprehension of the Universal Mind. We individuals approach it through our own mistakes and blunders, through our accumulated experience, through our illumined consciousness—how, otherwise, can we know Truth?

E.: I cannot prove scientifically that truth must be conceived as a truth that is valid independent of humanity; but I believe it firmly. I believe, for instance, that the Pythagorean theorem in geometry states something that is approximately true, independent of the existence of man. Anyway, if there is a *reality* independent of man there is also a truth relative to this reality; and in the same way the negation of the first engenders a negation of the existence of the latter.

T.: Truth, which is one with the Universal Being, must essentially be human, otherwise whatever we individuals realize as true can never be called truth—at least the truth which is described as scientific and can only be reached through the process of logic, in other words, by an organ of thoughts which is human. According to Indian Philosophy there is Brahman the absolute Truth, which cannot be conceived by the isolation of the individual mind or described by words, but can only be realized by completely merging the individual in its infinity. But such a truth cannot belong to Science. The nature of truth which we are discussing is an appearance—that is to say what appears to be true to the human mind and therefore is human, and may be called *máyá*, or illusion.

E.: So according to your conception, which may be the Indian conception, it is not the illusion of the individual, but of humanity as a whole.

T.: In science we go through the discipline of eliminating the personal limitations of our individual minds and thus reach that comprehension of truth which is in the mind of the Universal Man.

E.: The problem begins whether Truth is independent of our consciousness.

T.: What we call truth lies in the rational harmony between the subjective and objective aspects of reality, both of which belong to the super-personal man.

E.: Even in our everyday life we feel compelled to ascribe a reality independent of man to the objects we use. We do this to connect the experiences of our senses in a reasonable way. For instance, if nobody is in this house, yet that table remains where it is.

T.: Yes, it remains outside the individual mind, but not outside the universal mind. The table which I perceive is perceptible by the same kind of consciousness which I possess.

E.: Our natural point of view in regard to the existence of truth apart from humanity cannot be explained or proved, but it is a belief which nobody can lack—no primitive beings even. We attribute to Truth a super-human objectivity; it is indispensable for us, this reality which is independent for our existence and our experience and our mind—though we cannot say what it means.

T.: Science has proved that the table as a solid object is an appearance, and therefore that which the human mind perceives as a table would not exist if that mind were naught. At the same time it must be admitted that the fact, that the ultimate physical reality of the table is nothing but a multitude of separate revolving centres of electric forces, also belongs to the human mind.

In the apprehension of truth there is an eternal conflict between the universal human mind and the same mind confined in the individual. The perpetual process of reconciliation is being carried on in our science and philosophy, and in our ethics. In any case, if there be any truth absolutely unrelated to humanity then for us it is absolutely non-existing.

It is not difficult to imagine a mind to which the sequence of things happens not in space, but only in time like the sequence of notes in music. For such a mind its conception of reality is akin to the musical reality in which Pythagorean geometry can have no meaning. There is the reality of paper, infinitely different from the reality of literature. For the kind of mind possessed by the moth, which eats that paper, literature is absolutely non-existent, yet for Man's mind literature has a greater value of truth than the paper itself. In a similar manner, if there be some truth which has no sensuous or rational relation to the human mind it will ever remain as nothing so long as we remain human beings.

E.: Then I am more religious than you are!

T.: My religion is in the reconciliation of the Super-personal Man, the Universal human spirit, in my own individual being. This has been the subject of my Hibbert Lectures, which I have called "The Religion of Man".

Appendix III

Dadu and the Mystery of Form

(From an article in the *Visvabharati Quarterly* by
Professor Kshiti Mohan Sen.)

THE language of man has been mainly occupied with telling us
about the elements into which the finite world has been analysed; nevertheless, now and again, it reveals glimpses of the
world of the Infinite as well; for the spirit of man has discovered
rifts in the wall of Matter. Our intellect can count the petals,
classify the scent, and describe the colour of the rose, but its
unity finds its expression when we rejoice in it.

The intellect at best can give us only a broken view of things.
The marvellous vision of the Seer, in spite of the scoffing in
which both Science and Metaphysics so often indulge, can alone
make manifest to us the truth of a thing in its completeness.
When we thus gain a vision of unity, we are no longer intellectually aware of detail, counting, classifying, or distinguishing—
for then we have found admittance into the region of the spirit,
and there we simply measure the truth of our realization by the
intensity of our joy.

What is the meaning of this unutterable joy? That which we know by intellectual process is something outside ourselves. But the vision of anything in the fullness of its unity involves the realization of the unity of the self within, as well as of the relation between the two. The knowledge of the *many* may make us proud, but it makes us glad when our kinship with the *One* is brought home to us. Beauty is the name that we give to this acknowledgment of unity and of its relationship with ourselves.

It is through the beauty of Nature, or of Human Character, or Service, that we get our glimpses of the Supreme Soul whose essence is bliss. Or rather, it is when we become conscious of Him in Nature, or Art, or Service, that Beauty flashes out. And whenever we thus light upon the Dweller-within, all discord disappears and Love and Beauty are seen inseparable from Truth. It is really the coming of Truth to us as kinsman which floods our being with Joy.

This realization in Joy is immediate, self-sufficient, ultimate. When the self experiences Joy within, it is completely satisfied and has nothing more to ask from the outside world. Joy, as we know it, is a direct, synthetic measure of Beauty and neither awaits nor depends upon any analytical process. In our Joy, further, we behold not only the unity, but also the origin, for the Beauty which tells us of Him can be nothing but radiance reflected, melody re-echoed, from Him; else would all this have been unmeaning indeed—Society, Civilization, Humanity. The progress of Man would otherwise have ended in an orgy of the gratification of his animal passions.

The power of realization, for each particular individual, is limited. All do not attain the privilege of directly apprehending the universal Unity. Nevertheless, a partial vision of it, say in a flower, or in a friend, is a common experience; moreover, the potentiality is inherent in every individual soul, by dint of disciplined striving, to effect its own expansion and thereupon eventually to achieve the realization of the Supreme Soul.

By whom, meanwhile, are these ineffable tidings from the realm of the Spirit, the world of the Infinite, brought to us? Not by potentates or philosophers, but by the poor, the untutored, the despised. And with what superb assurance do they lead us out of the desert of the intellect into the paradise of the Spirit!

When our metaphysicians, dividing themselves into rival schools of Monism, Dualism or Monistic-Dualism, had joined together in dismissing the world as *Maya*, then, up from the depths of their social obscurity, rose these cobblers, weavers, and sewers of bags, proclaiming such theorems of the intellect to be all nonsense; for the metaphysicians had not seen with their own inner vision how the world overflowed with Truth and Love, Beauty and Joy.

Dadu, Ravidas, Kabir and Nanak were no ascetics; they bore no message of poverty, or renunciation, for their own sake; they were poets who had pierced the curtain of appearances and had glimpses of the world of Unity, where God himself is a poet. Their words cannot stand the glare of logical criticism; they babble, like babes, of the joy of their vision of Him, of the ecstasy into which His music has thrown them.

Nevertheless, it is they, not the scientists or philosophers, who have taught us of reality. On the one side the Supreme Soul is alone, on the other my individual soul is alone. If the two do not come together, then indeed there befalls the greatest of all calamities, the utter emptiness of chaos. For all the abundance of His inherent joy, God is in want of my joy of Him; and Reality in its perfection only blossoms where we meet.

"When I look upon the beauty of this Universe", says Dadu,

"I cannot help asking: 'How, O Lord, did you come to create it? What sudden wave of joy coursing through your being compelled its own manifestation? Was it really due to desire for self-expression, or simply on the impulse of emotion? Or was it perhaps just your fancy to revel in the play of form? Is this play then so delightful to you; or is it that you would see your own inborn delight thus take shape?' Oh how can these questions be answered in words?" cries Dadu. "Only those who know will understand."

"Why not go to him who has wrought this marvel", says Dadu elsewhere, "and ask: 'Cannot your own message make clear this wondrous making of the One into the many?' When I look on creation as beauty of form, I see only Form and Beauty. When I look on it as life, everywhere I see Life. When I see it in relation, it is of bewildering variety. When I see it in my own soul, all its variousness is merged in the beauty of the Supreme Soul. This eye of mine then becomes also the eye of Brahma, and in this exchange of mutual vision does Dadu behold Truth."

The eye cannot see the face—for that purpose a mirror is necessary. That is to say, either the face has to be put at a distance from the eye, or the eye moved away from the face—in any case what was one has to be made into two. The image is not the face itself, but how else is that to be seen?

So does God mirror Himself in Creation; and since He cannot place Himself outside His own Infinity, He can only gain a vision of Himself—and get a taste of His own joy—through my joy in Him and in His Universe. Hence the anxious striving of the devotee to keep himself thoroughly pure—not through any pride of puritanism, but because his soul is the playground where God would revel in Himself. Had not God's radiance, His beauty, thus found its form in the Universe, its joy in the devotee, He would have remained mere formless, colourless Being in the nothingness of infinity.

This is what makes the Mystery so profound, so inscrutable. Whether we say that only Brahma is true, or only the universe is true, we are equally far from the Truth, which can only be expressed as both *this* and *that*, or neither *this* nor *that*.

And Dadu can only hint at it by saying: "Neither death nor life is He; He neither goes out, nor does He come in; nor sleeps, nor wakes; nor wants, nor is satisfied. He is neither I nor you, neither One nor Two. For no sooner do I say that all is One, than I find us both; and when I say there are two, I see we're One. So, O Dadu, rest content to look on Him just as He is, in the deep of your heart, and give up wrestling with vain imaginings and empty words."

"Words shower", Dadu goes on, "when spouts the fount of the intellect; but where realization grows, there music has its seat." When the intellect confesses defeat, and words fail, then, indeed, from the depth of the heart wells up the song of the joy of realization. What words cannot make clear, melody can; to its strains one can revel in the vision of God in His revels.

"That is why", cries Dadu, "your universe, this creation of yours, has charmed me so—your waters and your breezes, and this earth which holds them, with its ranges of mountains, its great oceans, its snow—capped poles, its blazing sun, because, through all the three regions of earth, sky and heaven, amidst all their multifarious life, it is your ministration, your beauty, that keeps me enthralled. Who can know you, O Invisible, Unapproachable, Unfathomable! Dadu has no desire to know; he is satisfied to remain enraptured with all this beauty of yours, and to rejoice in it with you."

To look upon Form as the play of His love is not to belittle it. In creating the senses God did not intend them to be starved. "And so", says Dadu, "the eye is feasted with colour, the ear with music, the palate with flowers, wondrously provided." And we find that the body longs for the spirit, the spirit for the body; the flower for the scent, the scent for the flower; our words for truth, the Truth for words; form for its ideal, the idea for form; all thus mutual worship is but the worship of the ineffable Reality behind, by whose Presence every one of them is glorified. And Dadu struggles not, but simply keeps his heart open to this shower of love and thus rejoices in perpetual Springtime.

Every vessel of form the Formless fills with Himself, and in their beauty He gains them in return. With His love the Passionless fulfils every devoted heart and sets it a-dance, and their love streams back to the Colourless, variegated with the tints of each. Beauteous Creation yields up her charms, in all their purity, to her Lord. Need she make further protestation, in words of their mutual love? So Dadu surrenders his heart, mind and soul at the feet of his Beloved. His one care is that they be not sullied.

If any one should object that evanescent Form is not worthy to represent the Eternal, Dadu would answer that it is just because Form is fleeting that it is a help, not a hindrance, to His worship. While returning, back to its Origin, it captures our mind and takes it along with itself. The call of Beauty tells us of the Unthinkable, towards whom it lies. In passing over us, Death assures us of the truth of Life.

Appendix IV

An Address in the Chapel of Manchester College, Oxford, On Sunday, May 25, 1930, by Rabindranath Tagore

IN his early youth, stricken with a great sorrow at the death of his grandmother, my father painfully groped for truth when his world had darkened, and his life lost its meaning. At this moment of despair a torn page of a manuscript carried by a casual wind was brought to his notice. The text it contained was the first verse of the Ishopanishad:

> "Isavasyam idam survam
>   Yat Kincha jagatyam jagat,
> tena tyaktena bhunjitha
>   Ma grdhah Kasyasvitdhanam."

It may be thus translated:

"Thou must know that whatever moves in this moving world is enveloped by God. And therefore find thy enjoyment in renunciation, never coveting what belongs to others."

In this we are enjoined to realize that all facts that move and change have their significance in their relation to one everlasting truth. For then we can be rid of the greed of acquisition, gladly dedicating everything we have to that Supreme Truth. The change in our mind is immense in its generosity of expression when an utter sense of vanity and vacancy is relieved at the consciousness of a pervading reality.

I remember once while on a boat trip in a strange neighbourhood I found myself unexpectedly at the confluence of three great rivers as the daylight faded and the night darkened over a desolation dumb and inhospitable. A sense of dread possessed the crew and an oppressive anxiety burdened my thoughts with its unreasonable exaggeration all through the dark hours. The morning came and at once the brooding obsession vanished. Everything remained the same only the sky was filled with light.

The night had brought her peace, the peace of a black ultimatum in which all hope ceased in an abyss of nothingness, but the peace of the morning appeared like that of a mother's smile, which in its serene silence utters, "I am here". I realized why birds break out singing in the morning, and felt that their songs are their own glad answers to the emphatic assurance of a Yes in the morning light in which they find a luminous harmony of their own existence. Darkness drives our being into an isolation of insignificance and we are frightened because in the dark the sense of our own truth dwindles into a minimum. Within us we carry a positive truth, the consciousness of our personality, which naturally seeks from our surroundings its response in a truth which is positive, and then in this harmony we find our wealth of reality and are gladly ready to sacrifice. That which distinguishes man from the animal is the fact that he expresses himself not in his claims, in his needs, but in his sacrifice, which has the creative energy that builds his home, his society, his civilization. It proves that his instinct acknowledges the inexhaustible wealth of a positive truth which gives highest value to existence. In whatever we are mean, greedy and unscrupulous, there are the dark bands in the spectrum of our consciousness; they prove chasms of bankruptcy in our realization of the truth that the world moves, not in a blank sky of negation, but in the bosom of an ideal spirit of fulfilment.

Most often crimes are committed when it is night. It must not be thought that the only reason for this is that in the dark they are likely to remain undetected. But the deeper reason is that in the dark the negative aspect of time weakens the positive sense of our own humanity. Our victims, as well as we ourselves, are less real to us in the night, and that which we miss within we desperately seek outside us. Wherever in the human world the individual self forgets its isolation, the light that unifies is revealed the light of the Everlasting Yes, whose sound-symbol in India is OM. Then it becomes easy for man to be good not because his badness is restrained, but because of his joy in the positive background of his own reality, because his mind no longer dwells in a fathomless night of an anarchical world of denial.

Man finds an instance of this in the idea of his own country, which reveals to him a positive truth, the idea that has not the darkness of negation which is sinister, which generates suspicion, exaggerates fear, encourages uncontrolled greed; for his own country is an indubitable reality to him which delights his soul. In such intense consciousness of reality we discover our own greater self that spreads beyond our physical life and immediate present, and offers us generous opportunities of enjoyment in renunciation.

In the introductory chapter of our civilization individuals by some chance found themselves together within a geographic enclosure. But a mere crowd without an inner meaning of inter-relation is negative, and therefore it can easily be hurtful. The individual who is a mere component part of an unneighbourly crowd, who in his exclusiveness represents only himself, is apt to be suspicious of others, with no inner control in hating and hitting his fellow-beings at the very first sight. This savage mentality is the product of the barren spirit of negation that dwells in the spiritual night. But when the morning of mutual recognition broke out, the morning of co-operative life, that divine mystery which is the creative spirit of unity, imparted meaning to individuals in a larger truth named "people". These individuals gladly surrendered themselves to the realization of their true humanity, the humanity of a great wholeness composed of generations of men consciously and unconsciously building up a perfect future. They realized peace according to the degree of unity which they attained in their mutual relationship, and within that limit they found the one sublime truth which pervades time that moves, the things that change, the life that grows, the thoughts that flow onwards. They united with themselves the surrounding physical nature in her hills and rivers, in the dance of rhythm in all her forms and colours, in the blue of her sky, the tender green of her corn shoots.

In gradual degrees men became aware that the subtle

intricacies of human existence find their perfection in the harmony of interdependence, never in the vigorous exercise of elbows by a mutually pushing multitude, in the arrogant assertion of independence which fitly belongs to the barren rocks and deserts grey with the pallor of death.

For rampant individualism is against what is truly human—that is to say spiritual; it belongs to the primitive poverty of the animal life, it is the confinement of a cramped spirit, of restricted consciousness.

The limited boundaries of a race or a country within which the supreme truth of humanity has been more or less realized in the past are crossed to-day from the outside. The countries are physically brought closer to each other by science. But science has not brought with it the light that helps understanding. On the contrary science on its practical side has raised obstacles among them against the development of a sympathetic knowledge.

But I am not foolish enough to condemn science as materialistic. No truth can be that. Science means intellectual probity in our knowledge and dealings with the physical world and such conscientiousness has a spiritual quality that encourages sacrifice and martyrdom. But in science the oft-used half-truth that honesty is the best policy is completely made true and our mind's honesty in this field never fails to bring us the best profit for our living. Mischief finds its entry through this back-door of utility, tempting the primitive in man, arousing his evil passions. And through this the great meeting of races has been obscured of its great meaning. When I view it in my mind I am reminded of the fearful immensity of the meeting of the three mighty rivers where I found myself unprepared in a blackness of universal menace. Over the vast gathering of peoples the insensitive night darkly broods, the night of unreality. The primitive barbarity of limitless suspicion and mutual jealousy fills the world's atmosphere to-day—the barbarity of the aggressive individualism of nations, pitiless in its greed, unashamed of its boastful brutality.

Those that have come out for depredation in this universal night have the indecent audacity to say that such conditions are eternal in man, that the moral ideals are only for individuals but that the race belongs to the primitive nature of the animal.

But when we see that in the range of physical power man acknowledges no limits in his dreams, and is not even laughed at when he hopes to visit the neighbouring planet, must he insult his humanity by proclaiming that human nature has reached its limit of moral possibility? We must work with all our strength for the seemingly impossible; we must be sure that faith in the perfect builds the path for the perfect—that the external fact of unity which has surprised us must be sublimated in an internal truth of unity which would light up the Truth of Man the Eternal.

Nations are kept apart not merely by international jealousy, but also by their *Karma*, their own past, handicapped by the burden of the dead. They find it hard to think that the mentality which they fondly cultivated within the limits of a narrow past has no continuance in a wider future, they are never tired of uttering the blasphemy that warfare is eternal, that physical might has its inevitable right of moral cannibalism where the flesh is weak. The wrong that has been done in the past seeks to justify itself by its very perpetuation, like a disease by its chronic malignity, and it sneers and growls at the least proposal of its termination. Such an evil ghost of a persistent past, the dead that would cling to life, haunts the night to-day over mutually alienated countries, and men that are gathered together in the dark cannot see each other's faces and features.

We in India are unfortunate in not having the chance to give expression to the best in us in creating intimate relations with the powerful nations, whose preparations are all leading to an enormous waste of resources in a competition of brow-beating and bluff. Some great voice is waiting to be heard which will usher in the sacred light of truth in the dark hours of the nightmare of politics, the voice which will proclaim that "God is over all", and exhort us never to covet, to be great in renunciation that gives us the wealth of spirit, strength of truth, leads us from the illusion of power to the fullness of perfection, to the *Santam*, who is peace eternal, to the *Advaitam*, who is the infinite One in the heart of the manifold. But we in India have not yet had the chance. Yet we have our own human voice which truth demands. The messengers of truth have ever joined hands across centuries, across the seas, across historical barriers, and they help to raise up the great continent of human brotherhood from *avidya*, from the slimy bottom of spiritual apathy. We individuals, however small may be our power and whatever corner of the world we may belong to, have a claim upon us to add to the light of the consciousness that comprehends all humanity. And for this cause I ask your co-operation, not only because co-operation gives us strength in our work, but because co-operation itself is the best aspect of the truth we represent; it is an end and not merely the means.

Let us keep our faith firm in the objectivity of the source of our spiritual ideal of unity, though it cannot be proved by any mathematical logic. Let us proclaim in our conduct that it has already been given to us to be realized, like a song which has only to be mastered and sung, like the morning which has only to be welcomed by raising the screens, opening the doors.

The idea of a millennium is treasured in our ancient legends. The instinct cradled and nourished in them has profound meaning. It is like the instinct of a chick which dimly feels that an infinite world of freedom *is* already given to it, truer than the narrow fact of its immediate life within the egg. An agnostic chick has the rational right to doubt it, but at the same time it cannot help pecking at its shell. The human soul, confined in its limitation, has also dreamt of millennium, and striven for a spiritual emancipation which seems impossible of attainment, and yet it feels its reverence for some ever-present source of inspiration in which all its experience of the true, the good and beautiful finds its reality.

And therefore it has been said by the Upanishad: "Thou must know that God pervades all things that move and change in this moving world; find thy enjoyment in renunciation, covet not what belongs to others."

> "Ya eko varno bahudha saktiyogat
> Varnan anekan nihitartho dadhati.
> Vichaiti chante visvamadau sa devah
> Sa no buddhya subhaya samyunaktu."

He who is one, and who dispenses the inherent needs of all peoples and all times, who is in the beginning and the end of all things, may He unite us with the bond of truth, of common fellowship, of righteousness.

Index

Biography

Rabindranath Tagore (1861-1941) was the youngest son of Debendranath Tagore, a leader of the Brahmo Samaj, which was a new religious sect in nineteenth-century Bengal and which attempted a revival of the ultimate monistic basis of Hinduism as laid down in the *Upanishads*. He was educated at home; and although at seventeen he was sent to England for formal schooling, he did not finish his studies there. In his mature years, in addition to his many-sided literary activities, he managed the family estates, a project which brought him into close touch with common humanity and increased his interest in social reforms. He also started an experimental school at Shantiniketan where he tried his Upanishadic ideals of education. From time to time he participated in the Indian nationalist movement, though in his own non-sentimental and visionary way; and Gandhi, the political father of modern India, was his devoted friend. Tagore was knighted by the ruling British Government in 1915, but within a few years he resigned the honour as a protest against British policies in India.

Tagore had early success as a writer in his native Bengal. With his translations of some of his poems he became rapidly known in the West. In fact his fame attained a luminous height, taking him across continents on lecture tours and tours of friendship. For the world he became the voice of India's spiritual heritage; and for India, especially for Bengal, he became a great living institution.

Although Tagore wrote successfully in all literary genres, he was first of all a poet. Among his fifty and odd volumes of poetry are *Manasi* (1890) [The Ideal One], *Sonar Tari* (1894) [The Golden Boat], *Gitanjali* (1910) [Song Offerings], *Gitimalya* (1914) [Wreath of Songs], and *Balaka* (1916) [The Flight of Cranes]. The English renderings of his poetry, which include *The Gardener* (1913), *Fruit-Gathering* (1916), and *The Fugitive* (1921), do not generally correspond to particular volumes in the original Bengali; and in spite of its title, *Gitanjali: Song Offerings* (1912), the most acclaimed of them, contains poems from other works besides its namesake. Tagore's major plays are *Raja* (1910) [The King of the Dark Chamber], *Dakghar* (1912) [The Post Office], *Achalayatan* (1912) [The Immovable], *Muktadhara* (1922) [The Waterfall], and *Raktakaravi* (1926) [Red Oleanders]. He is the author of several volumes of short stories and a number of novels, among them *Gora* (1910), *Ghare-Baire* (1916) [The Home and the World], and *Yogayog* (1929) [Crosscurrents]. Besides these, he wrote musical dramas, dance dramas, essays of all types, travel diaries, and two autobiographies, one in his middle years and the other shortly before his death in 1941. Tagore also left numerous drawings and paintings, and songs for which he wrote the music himself.

This autobiography/biography was written at the time of the award and first published in the book series Les Prix Nobel. *It was later edited and republished in* Nobel Lectures.

CPSIA information can be obtained
at www.ICGtesting.com
Printed in the USA
JSHW032202181221
21378JS00001B/1